MY KIDS GROW
AND SO DO I

MY KIDS GROW AND SO DO I

A PARENT'S TOOLBOX FOR PRACTICAL SPIRITUALITY

JOHANNA VAN ZWET

Ascad Communications

Excerpts from the Bible were taken from either the Oxford New English Bible or the Every Day Bible.

Quotations from "Your Life. Why It Is the Way It Is and What You Can Do About It", by Bruce McArthur, 1993, have been reprinted with courtesy of A.R.E. Press.
Quotations from the Edgar Cayce Readings have been adapted to modern day English.

Ascad Communications, Inc.
15732 Los Gatos Blvd. #306
Los Gatos, CA 95030, USA

First edition.

Manufactured in the United States of America. Printed in Poland.
10 9 8 7 5 4 3 2

Designed by Bruce McMullen

Library of Congress Catalog Card Number: 96-085592

Van Zwet, Johanna
    My kids grow and so do I: a parent's toolbox for practical spirituality
/by Johanna van Zwet.
            p. cm.
    Includes bibliographical references and index.
ISBN 0-9653566-0-4
    1. Spiritual life - family. 2. Parenting. I. Title.

131-dc20

96-085592

Attention organizations, colleges, universities and schools: Quantity discounts are available on bulk purchases of this book for educational training purposes, fund raising, or gift giving. Special books, booklets, or book excerpts can also be created to fit your specific needs. For information, please contact the publisher. For individual purchases please refer to the order form at the back of the book.

To my mother, Margaretha Sillevis Smitt,
with love, respect and gratitude.

CONTENTS

ACKNOWLEDGMENTS

When this book was still a growing manuscript my sister Lizet remarked at one point: "This is a common creation", meaning: these ideas are out there and people everywhere are picking them up. I just happened to write them down. I think she is right. As parents reflect on these matters more and more and apply what they know, these ideas become accessible to others, and thus to me, the scribe. I would like to thank all who have committed themselves to finding out who we parents are, what we are about, and why we are here.

I thank the many parents with whom I have come into contact over the years and who have shared their life, love and friendship with me. I learned from each of them. In particular I thank Suzie Wall, Julie Groves and Valerie Lozowicki for their friendship and their valuable feedback and encouragement. I thank Jo-Anne Van der Vat-Chromy, Linda Nanez and Shirley Skellenger for their comments on the manuscript.

My thanks go to my husband, Antek, who, in times of uncertainty, makes sure the lights in the tunnel are on. And to my sister Lizet, who can always be counted upon to jolt the porcelain cabinet with new and unexpected ideas.
Last but not least my thanks go to my sons Mark, Jesse and Alan, bringers of love, hope, and never ending challenges!

PROLOGUE

This book is the natural result of a decade of living with small, growing children. After I gave birth to our first baby, my daily life consisted of caring for first one, then two, then three little children: meeting their physical as well as their emotional, social and intellectual needs. I searched for ways to improve my parenting skills. I took classes, read books and talked to other parents. I felt the need to educate myself in the area of child rearing and psychology, and I read many volumes pertaining to children, their development and education. I read material dealing with problem solving techniques and tested the ones that appealed to me and then incorporated the ones that seemed to work.

At some time during my early parenting years an awareness of profound gratitude started to grow in me. The feeling of intense joy would at times wash over me, leaving me walking on clouds and at the same time puzzled. Puzzled because there was nothing I had done previously in my life that would make me more deserving of a bunch of happy, healthy tykes than any other person. Yet, with no apparent justification, there they were, placed in my husband's and my care. I felt that other causes and motivations had to be at play. A hidden reality, different from the one I was perceiving, had to be operating to have it all make sense. Thus my curiosity in spiritual matters was aroused.

After tucking in the kids at night, and if I still had the energy, I would read all the books and material I could lay my hands on relating to spiritual life. I read books about mysticism, meditation and prayer, inner guidance and dreams, reincarnation and karma. I invited into my house two Jehovah's witnesses to explain to me their life's dedication, and I read all the material they left with me. I read "Christ Among Us" (by Anthony J. Wilhelm), a presentation of the Catholic faith. I read fundamentalist material, new age material, channeled material, works by Billy Graham. I read books about the life and work of Edgar Cayce, an American psychic, books by Joel Goldsmith, an American mystic, and I explored "A Course in Miracles". These sources began to quench my thirst for knowledge about the spiritual aspect of my being.

For some time I continued on these separate tracks: gaining insight in child rearing during the day and in personal spiritual development during the evening. It was inevitable that at one point I should connect the two: to apply in the life I shared with my children the spiritual knowledge gained.

To me my daily life with its score of little chores and jobs, its small and large frustrations and irritations turned into a playing field. Life as a mom of small children became a field in which I could explore, test and apply the newly found spiritual insights. Once I had made the connection, I began to see what a great opportunity parenting is for spiritual development. While living with my growing children I noticed the huge difference it makes when parenting is done from a new perspective, namely as an opportunity for personal growth. The difference is in the broader perspective in which daily tasks are placed. The difference is in the sense of purpose and peace of mind that this new perspective brings.

The motivation to write a book about the spiritual life of parents stems from my own attempts to find a book on this subject. The book would have to deal with spiritual life practiced and developed in the busy and very physical life of a parent of small children. On many occasions I felt the need for a book like that and did not find any. Knowing from experience that others in similar situations face similar questions, I plucked up the courage and started to write. I put down my experiences past and present, as well as insights and perspectives gained over the years.

While in the process of putting down my thoughts in words I realized that writing this guidebook answered to a personal need as well. After spending more than a decade of my life as a parent and full time homemaker, writing this book in a way resembles writing a thesis at the end of one's studies. It reflects the work and commitment dedicated to a field of interest.

This book records the steps I took as a young mother of three. It is the story of the awareness, emerging gradually, that being a parent is a great opportunity to grow as a person. It also tells of the "ups and doubts" of my journey. I imagined that I was writing a letter to a friend who has just become a parent and who has asked me to tell of my experiences. Please accept these words from a friend, a fellow traveler.

INTRODUCTION

Mom and dad are meditating. With eyes closed, they are quietly and rhythmically breathing in and breathing out. They are waiting to be transported to ever further reaches of the mind. But where are the kids? Well, they're tearing down the house! Surely there must be a better way to live a spiritual life and raise a family at the same time.

How can the practical world of child rearing be reconciled with the lofty realm of spirituality? You might argue that parenting is such a practical and busy occupation, that there is neither time nor place for transcendent thinking. And that spirituality with its skyscraping concepts does not seem to have anything to offer parents. Well, look at it this way: You are a three dimensional being. You are body, mind and spirit. These three levels of your being are not isolated from each other. Together they form who you are. You express yourself on the physical, mental and spiritual level, as do your children. To get clarity into parenting issues you need to look at all three levels. It is not enough to only take the physical reality (consisting of the people and things around you and activities you engage in) and mental reality (motivation, planning, goal setting, psychology, group dynamics, etc.) into account. You need to include the spiritual reality in your view. Spiritual reality is the world where the spark of an idea originates, it is the world where intention plays a key role and where ideals are landmarks.

But most of all, it is the realm where Love is recognized as the essence of Life. The key to reconcile the earthly occupation of child rearing with spirituality is in the practical application of spiritual concepts in the parent-child relationship. In the application of what you know to be true you will find spiritual growth.

The sub-title to this book is "A Parent's Toolbox For Practical Spirituality." This book will introduce a variety of spiritual tools. They will help you apply spirituality in daily life and thus help you brave the many challenges of parenthood. Practical spirituality can be brought to bear on many issues facing families today. With practical spirituality it is no longer necessary to separate the explorations of your inner life from the demands you face as a parent. You do not have to leave the kids to their own counsel in order to retreat into your inner space. On the contrary. When you see in parenting an opportunity to apply what you know to be true spiritually, your children's needs will not impinge on your own. Instead their needs will become calls to turn within and consult your inner wisdom right at the moment you need it most.

The single most important step towards expressing spirituality in practice is to become aware of the intent that forms the basis of your life. Once you know your life's intent, in this book called the *spiritual ideal*[1], you can

---

[1] The concept of spiritual ideals and the setting of ideals can be found in books about the life and work of Edgar Cayce. Edgar Cayce (1877-1945) was an American psychic who, in the course of forty years, gave over 14,000 readings to thousands of individuals in response to questions about physical ailments, mental concerns and spiritual needs. His readings are conserved and studied by the Association for Research and Enlightenment (A.R.E.), P.O.Box 656, Virginia Beach, VA 23451-0656, a membership organization.

learn to express that ideal in thoughts and attitudes as well as in decisions and activities.

The first three chapters will guide you to discover your spiritual ideal, your life's intent. You will see how to translate your spiritual ideal into new attitudes and new actions regarding your children. Thus the setting of ideals becomes a tool that enables you to express in daily life with kids what is most important to you, namely the truth you hold in the center of your being. Like a compass, the framework of ideals allows you to set your course and gives you feedback on your progress. The second chapter offers a step by step process of defining your ideal and the attitudes and actions naturally flowing from it. And the many examples of Chapter 3 will help you along the way.

Chapters 4 through 7 discuss the ways in which to nurture your inner life. An active and vibrant inner life is essential for experiencing inner peace. The instruments of prayer, meditation and consulting inner guidance enable you to turn within. These three tools allow you to discover the wealth spiritual life has to offer.

Chapters 8, 9 and 10 deal with the practical application of spirituality in the parent-child relationship. They discuss how spiritual tools, described in earlier chapters, can help you deal with common situations like disagreements, fights, demands, tough choices, illness and more. You will see how you break down nebulous spiritual concepts into practical objective results regarding the relationship between you and your child. You learn how to consciously connect who you are with what you do. When your heart's intent becomes visible through the work of your hands, you are on your way to wholeness.

Finally, each chapter concludes with a section called "Application." The purpose of this section is to help you get started to think about the concepts presented in the chapter in personal terms. (In chapters 9 and 10 "Application" sections appear throughout the text, where applicable.) When reading an "Application" section you might find it convenient to have a notebook and pen handy to record your thoughts. These "Application" sections aim at involving you actively, thus bridging the gap between thought and application, between theory and practice. For in the application of what you know to be true you find the key to spiritual growth.

Throughout the book the pronouns "she" and "he" are used in turn when referring to a child in general.

1

PARENTS AND SPIRITUALITY

*The eternal question that runs through life is
this: What is truly valuable in thought, in
activity, and in experience? Only from within
can come a stable estimate of what is
worthwhile.*

Edgar Cayce

WHAT DOES SPIRITUALITY HAVE TO OFFER PARENTS?

The arrival of children is one of the most defining
moments in a person's life. From now on there is a new
player in the field, who will make sure that she is taken
into account. Life is irrevocably changed. Things are
never the same again. And "things" include practically
everything: from daily routines and habits, to feelings and
emotions, from attitudes and priorities to the relationship
of the parents and their relationship with everybody else.
The coming of still more children will only magnify this
effect and make the degree of life changes even greater.

To paint a picture of an ordinary day of any parent you only have to think of the following combination in one day. A deadline at work, a visit to the dentist with the kids, soccer practice and carpool, dinner, kids in the tub and bedtime, followed by a parent-teacher meeting at school. Parenting is a balancing act while juggling ever so many needs. The needs of the kids and of the partner, of oneself, of providing a living, of maintaining a stable family life, of functioning in a social circle. And that is only the beginning of the list. The emotional strain of dealing with growing children on a daily basis can at times be overwhelming. Few have experienced heights of happiness and depths of despair of this magnitude and in this frequency ever before. Is it any wonder that parents become stressed, that they lose perspective, or simply throw in the towel? Parents need a place to turn to, a place to retreat, to find new energy and vision. This is not about a health club or a get-away. This is about finding inspiration right in the middle of it all: the diapers, the tantrums, the carpool and the laundry.

The way to find peace of mind and purpose is to look for strength and vision to come from your inner being. The place to find new energy and vision is within. It is there that you are connected to the Source of Life. You can consciously choose to open yourself to let Life flow through your inner being, outward, toward the people and conditions around you. You can accomplish anything that is asked of you as long as the life line with the Source of Life is vibrant and strong.

Not just parents can choose to do this, anybody can. But parenthood is a beautiful opportunity to develop inner life. It confronts you with the stress of an endless stream of demands, needs and chores, as well as offers you a first row seat to experience the beauty of Creation. You may be too overwhelmed by the first part, the pressures, to even notice the second part, the beauty, if you do not find inner peace at the center of your life. The way to find peace of mind and purpose in the thick of it all is to turn within and recognize in parenting an opportunity for personal spiritual growth.

The children you bear present you with the opportunity to leave your old self behind and to grow spiritually. Parenting is not just a job one is performing, or an assignment that you need to accomplish successfully. Parenting is a way of being. It is a way of being that transforms. As your children develop their bodies and sharpen their minds, you, the parent, are challenged to turn within for guidance and peace. While guiding your growing children you can grow, too.

THREE WAYS TO LOOK AT PARENTING ISSUES

So here you are, parent of your children, unexpectedly faced with a range of questions, problems, issues and decisions you could never have dreamed of before. If you do not find a way to respond effectively to matters that come up daily, and even hourly, life with kids will overtake you and leave you bewildered and exhausted. Let's examine the various levels on which issues present themselves to parents.

On the physical level there is the environment you need to adjust to make life with a growing baby safe. You arrange a place for the baby to sleep, like a crib or bassinet. If space permits you might even set aside a bedroom and decorate it as a nursery. In the kitchen and living room you make sure that a crawling and toddling child will not get hurt or otherwise get into trouble. Breakables are put away, plants are taken to higher places, electrical outlets are sealed with childproof plugs. Moreover, physical care includes feeding, holding, bathing and the like. Various gadgets, tools and instruments like diapers, highchair, playpen, toys, car seat, medicine, etc. assist to make parenting as easy going as possible. All these measures, and more, are ways to meet physical demands that life with a newborn places on you. Many actually love this part of parenting and go all out in their preparations and purchases. Most of us in the western world are able to meet the basics of these physical needs of our children. An adjusted environment and physical care are indispensable. But they are not the only areas where parents are expected to respond effectively.

On the mental level various situations come up that you need to deal with, too. This is the level of organization and planning. It is the level of thoughts, convictions, policies, as well as encouragement, commitment, perseverance. On the mental level as well there are "instruments" that help parents cope with everyday occurrences. Parents rely on planning, routines and habits to let daily life run along more or less predictable lines. Your days would surely become chaotic if you did not have at least a general idea of how you are going to take care of the various tasks relating to your babies and children. People of course vary in their need to plan ahead or to rely on routines. It may be clear though, that some degree of planning is necessary. Coming to the breakfast table with a hungry and fussy infant serves no purpose. It's better to nurse the baby ahead of time.

Getting the baby ready for a bath only to find the tub still full of children's toys and yesterday's grime is frustrating and denies you the enjoyment of bathing time. Here also, first things first. Of course I don't have to tell you how you feel when your toddler just soiled the last clean diaper in the house! Better be prepared for that one, or else ... Apart from routines and planning, on the mental level there are other issues. It is important to gain knowledge in the areas of child development, psychology and pedagogy. Insight in these matters is indispensable to becoming an effective partner to your child. Some people seem to have a natural talent to interact soundly with children; others need to educate themselves. To deal with matters like sibling rivalry, disobedience, lying, etc., you can rely on behavioral techniques, subject of many a book on child rearing. In the bibliography you will find the titles of several books that offer sensible and practical suggestions to deal with issues that are part of the parent-child relationship. Until your youngest child enters kindergarten, working on these two levels, the purely physical level and the mental level, will take up most of the time you spend with them. You are busy with their physical needs and with emotional, intellectual and social issues concerning your children.

Solving little and big problems facing you, your children and your family as a whole is always challenging. And at times it can be overwhelming. The amount of work that needs to be done can be staggering. Moreover, if despite your honest efforts you cannot resolve a certain issue facing you and your children, it is hard not to become desperate or depressed. Add to that the fact that children have a way of taking their parents to the very limit, and it becomes clear that you cannot solve all problems with answers of a physical or mental nature. To get a new perspective on child rearing and its various facets, it helps to look for a reality beyond the purely physical and mental realities: the spiritual reality. This does not mean that a certain problem, like disobedience or whining, fits into a single category - physical, mental or spiritual. No, circumstances and experiences are integrated phenomena. The essence of an experience finds expression on various levels at the same time. There are several mutually non-exclusive ways to look at an occurrence. Only for the purpose of understanding the situation, is it helpful to distinguish between the various aspects. To gain a broader perspective on a certain parenting issue it helps to distinguish between levels of reality on which issues become manifest: the physical reality, the mental reality and the spiritual reality.

Life's spiritual reality is the basis. It does not make the physical and mental realities any less, it only places them in the right perspective. When facing an ordinary problem, you can let yourself be guided by what you know or sense to be a spiritual reality beyond the appearance of the problem. Reaching for a spiritual viewpoint and gaining spiritual insight helps greatly in obtaining and keeping peace of mind in the hustle and bustle that is a parent's life.

An everyday example of this is the insistent whining of a child. Children that whine feel like mosquitoes in midsummer. They keep on buzzing in your ear and there is no escape! In the case of whining it helps to distinguish among the three levels of reality. On the first level, the physical level, it looks as if the child needs a nap or is just being a nuisance. Responding on this level would be to put her to bed, or to send her to her room. Thus, you teach her that whining is not a socially acceptable behavior and results in separation. If you spank the child in an effort to let her "snap out" of her mood, you risk an even greater emotional upset, both on the part of the child as on your own. Moreover, the example you then give will teach the child that annoyance needs a physical response: just kick it out of your life. Clearly an adequate response to whining cannot always be found solely on the physical level.

Looking at it from the second level, the mental level, it becomes clear that having house rules helps greatly in reducing whining to a minimum. Also setting clear boundaries to behavior that is acceptable and being consistent about them is paramount. Discipline and house rules belong to the mental level. In the bibliography you will find titles of books that offer help in this area. For instance, Nancy Samalin's book "Loving Your Child Is Not Enough. Positive Discipline that Works" abounds with examples of how to handle problem spots in the parent-child relationship. These examples show clearly how to effectively deal with problems from the mental level, like disobedience, anger, sibling fights, etc.

However, whining can be the symptom of something else as well. Looked at from the third level, the spiritual level, you could interpret whining as a call for love, a call to connect to the parent's life. Consider the background to this statement. In the beginning, when the child is still in the mother's womb, mother and child are physically totally connected. The unborn baby and her mother are one. After the birth of the baby, the connection, although not continuous any more, is still very intensive: nursing, holding, cuddling, etc. The infant's cry, if not caused by some physical discomfort, is an expression of the need to connect again with the parent. And especially when the cause is physical discomfort, then the presence of a parent can be an ointment to the child's soul. When the child is a little older she will try to engage the parents to play and to enter her world. A parent who answers this call will receive as a reward the love the child returns and the child's contagious wonder for life. The child longs to feel the love of the parent. If the parent withholds her love, the child will start prodding and whining. The child does not know how to show her need to connect with the parent in an alternative or socially more acceptable way. It is up to the parent to recognize the child's "negative" behavior and reinterpret the appearance of a whine as a call for connection.

When you face a whining child, as all parents do at times, it helps to distinguish between levels of reality. Decide whether the problem is basically a physical one (e.g., lack of sleep), a mental one (e.g., lack of clear boundaries of behavior) or a spiritual one (call for love). In the last case it is up to you, the parent, to offer the child the love it needs in the form that fits the situation.

In the area of child rearing, where you meet with new and unexpected issues all the time, it is helpful to gain as complete an understanding of an issue as possible. You do this by recognizing that in the three dimensional world of body, mind and spirit, you experience life on three levels: the physical, the mental and the spiritual level. This means you have to expand your view of the world and of your life as a parent. When considering a problem or an issue in the family, you need to include the spiritual perspective.

CHOOSING TO LIVE LIFE SPIRITUALLY

How do you start to see life from a spiritual perspective? How do you learn to look for the spiritual reality behind everyday appearances? The first thing that comes to mind is to read about spiritual life. Read, explore, discuss and listen, those are the first steps. But the accumulation of facts and theories of itself is not a life changer. Change comes when you start to apply what you have learned. Application is the key word. In the application of what you know to be true you will find spiritual growth.

Because this is such an important principle, I would like to tell you about my experiences to illustrate this. When I started to become interested in spirituality I began to see the arrival of our children in a totally different light. Before, I considered them wonderful additions to our life, nicely planned and fitting into the way of life we controlled. Now, however, I began to see them more and more as messengers, fellow seekers, equal souls, coming to us by their own choice. Another example is the new way in which I started to approach so called problem situations. I learned to anticipate and "program" myself ahead of time to respond in an alternative way. I learned to release familiar attitudes and emotions like apprehension, anxiety and frustration. And then, right on the spot and right on the moment of engagement so to speak, to say a quick silent prayer asking Spirit (or God, if you will) to take the lead. (In Chapters 4 through 7 you will read more about this method of letting the Spirit do the work.) However, even as I started to have a different perspective on some of my life's situations, changes were incidental. A totally new outlook on life as a whole began to dawn on me when I started to get clarity into the purpose of my life here on earth. That awareness helped me pull together the incidental shifts and changes into a unified integral movement. Where before I had heard some very pleasant sounding individual notes, I now began to distinguish a melody.

Would we not all want to know why we are here? What is it exactly that we are supposed to be or to accomplish while in this earthly state? And what does parenting have to do with it all? The reason the answers to these questions seem so elusive, is that they are different for each person. Moreover, they have a way of growing over time, of evolving with a person. In short, the answers cannot be pinned down. However, to get a feel for, or maybe even a grip on your answers to questions about your life and purpose, there is a tool available to you, called the *spiritual ideal.* By defining and applying your spiritual ideal you work toward finding your answers to questions about your life here on earth.

YOUR SPIRITUAL IDEAL, YOUR COMPASS

A spiritual ideal is a thought that to you represents the highest understanding of truth and purpose in your life. It is the highest standard you can imagine yourself to meet. It is not an idea or a goal that you attain and then replace or forget. It is a thought belonging to the spiritual realm and it is individual in the sense that it fits you perfectly. It is something you aspire to and at the same time already hold within you. By consciously reaching for it, you take the first step on the road to making that quality a conscious part of you. Your spiritual ideal will be your compass that allows you to set a course and gives you feedback on your progress. It will become the standard against which you measure the quality of your life. It becomes the yardstick with which to measure your success, your happiness and peace. Your spiritual ideal forms the foundation of your house, the base of your painting, the 'basso continuo' of your music. Your individual spiritual ideal offers you the opportunity to get a feel for the essence of your life. And it will show you which attitudes and actions will bring you in touch with that essence.

To work with a spiritual ideal is to live it day to day. This means that you   shift emphasis from outcome to intent. Your attitudes and intentions become the focal point, rather than some defined objective result.   This is quite a change   from the perspective the western world typically promotes, with its focus on size of bank account, social standing, possessions, good looks, etc.

After defining your individual spiritual ideal you need to translate that ideal into   mental terms as well   as physical terms.   You are, after all, a three dimensional being, consisting of spirit, mind and body. To make your spiritual ideal a unifying positive force in your life, you need to address your mental and physical realities as well. From the one spiritual ideal the mental and physical ideals flow naturally. Thus a framework is established that connects the inner world (Spirit) through the intermediary (mind) with the physical outer world and your interaction with other people. That very connection is what makes a person whole.   Living your individual   spiritual ideal makes you whole and gives you direction. Applying your ideals forges who you are with what you do. The following example shows you how it works:

Carol has decided she wants to work with a spiritual ideal. At first she chooses *Show unconditional love.* She is the mother of three children, works part time as a receptionist and enjoys playing music and working in the yard. She recognizes that she especially loves children, she gets a kick out of being around them. Moreover, she has a natural way with children, and they feel her empathy with them. To specify her spiritual ideal a little more, and make it more workable, she decides to name it *Guide children.* At first this may sound vague and uncommitted, but the steps that follow this initial step will show otherwise.

With this central idea in the back of her mind Carol considers her children and formulates what her ideal attitude towards them would be in light of her newly found spiritual ideal. She decides to *Practice patience and tolerance,* which now has become her mental ideal in the area of her contact with her children. To make her mental ideal workable as well as measurable she needs to take the next step, namely to practice patience and tolerance in daily life, during the daily routines. One difficult spot in her daily life with her kids is at the end of the day when everyone is tired and wants to be left alone, but various things still need to be done. Thinking about this particular recurring situation she decides to apply her spiritual ideal *Guide children* (through her mental ideal *Practice patience and tolerance)* and she intends to do the following:

- *She will postpone doing the dishes till after the kids are asleep*

- *During bath time she will stay focused on the kids and not get distracted by other matters*

*- She will stick to one story and one song per child at bed-
time and be firm about it*

Thus Carol has formulated her physical ideals flowing
from her mental ideal, which in turn flows from her one
spiritual ideal. She has now set up a framework to
express what she holds dearly, namely children and
guiding them, in her day to day life. Working along the
same lines she considers another area of her daily life,
namely school and church. First she defines mental ideals
and then physical ideals that flow from these. Her mental
ideal in the area of school and church becomes: *Be
open to opportunities to work with groups of children.*
Flowing from this her physical ideals become:

*- Inquire at church and school if they are interested in her
setting up a music program*

- Have kids' friends over for a music and story time

- Enlist to help with fundraising for local teen center

She works likewise with the next area she considers, her
neighborhood. She decides to phrase her mental ideal as
follows: *Bring hope to the troubled teen next door.* And
the physical ideals flowing from this are:

- Ask if the teen needs a job working in the yard

*- Try to get the teen interested in preparations for teen
center*

Carol has her work cut out for her. As in her first work
area, her own children, she is finding a way to express
what she holds dearly in situations close to home: school,
church, neighborhood. The spiritual ideal *Guide*

children, that at first sounded vague and general, has directed her to some very practicable applications.

When working with her set of ideals for some time, Carol may want to adjust the wording to reflect either a changing situation or a shifting, clearer intent. The flexible framework of ideals is like a custom made compass. It is a tool that enables her to apply in daily life what she knows to be true in her heart.

To sum it up, the key things you can do to consciously live life from a spiritual perspective, mentioned so far, are:

- Get informed about spiritual matters

- Apply what you know to be true

- Set your compass: set your spiritual, mental and physical ideals, and live them

These three key elements form the basis of spiritual life and growth, and they are the subject of the following two chapters. The fourth key to spiritual life, turning within, is just as important. Chapters 4 through 7 discuss turning within and the development of inner life.

APPLICATION

1. As a parent have you experienced extremes in happiness and despair? Try to recall instances when you felt overjoyed in parenthood.

2. Write about times or issues relating to you and your child that have left you utterly desperate.

3. What is your customary way to deal with an experience like that? Yell - cry - get physical - retreat - send child away - punish - accuse - wait and see, etc. Do not become embarrassed by your answer. All parents face trying challenges and most of us do the best we can. Try to identify what your "the best you can"-response has been up to now. Only when you know where you stand now will you be able to consciously move ahead.

4. In your own life with your children can you identify several issues or situations that have a clear physical aspect? Examples:

   – Take infant to medical check-up
   – Arrange a baby-sitter for an evening out
   – Vacuum nursery room

5. Now try to identify activities or situations that have a clear mental aspect. Examples:

   – Planning things to bring along for the kids on a long drive
   – Teach kids to take turns in their play
   – Before bed time, instead of letting your child watch cartoons on TV, you read a story to settle the child down for the night

6. Can you think of an example in life with your children where the spiritual aspect comes to the fore? Examples:

   - Despite multiple warnings your child touches the wet paint with her finger and leaves a mark - This is not caused by lack of control of bodily movements (physical explanation). Nor is it an act of blatant disobedience (mental explanation). It is the expression of the urge to connect with *all* aspects of Creation.
   - Your child brings you a flower - Giving, sharing.
   - Your child is furious and screams when asked to interrupt play and clean up to come to dinner - Playing is creating. It is the child's way of learning and getting to know the world around her, and to being one with it. In play, she reaches for a balance of exchange with the world around her. When a call for dinner comes right at the time she is about to reach this balance, it can be very disturbing.

7. Do you feel like learning more about the spiritual aspect of your being? Are there sections on religion, metaphysics or mysticism in your home town library? Does your church offer programs for people interested in prayer, meditation or contemplation and Bible study?

Be fastidious in your choice of information and follow your "gut feeling" when choosing among sources. Allow yourself room to let new insights take root in you, before adding new concepts. These things cannot be rushed. Compare it to learning how to swim. You start at the shallow end and progress stroke by stroke. You learn by applying what you know so far.

2

THE SETTING OF IDEALS

—

STEP BY STEP

*The most important experience of this or any
person is to first know what is the ideal -
spiritually*

Edgar Cayce

YEARNING TO BE CONNECTED

Much of our culture's artistic expression evolves
around the theme of love in its various forms. The ever
recurring theme of romantic love of lovers is subject of
many a play, movie and song. Other aspects of love as
well, such as parental love, love and (loyalty) among
friends, fidelity, faithfulness, commitment, form the
threads that are woven into the fabric of countless stories
that have become classics: Orpheus in the Underworld,
Romeo and Juliet, Bambi, to name just a few. The national

hymn, The Star Spangled Banner, really is an ode to the loyalty and perseverance of a group of kindred souls working toward a common vision of freedom and justice. Here, as in many other artistic expressions, the other side of the coin finds a place as well: violence, death, brutality, rejection. In their plays, movies and songs, writers of all ages have tried to express the yearning for brotherhood, solidarity and love, the longing for perfection and purity. The reason these stories have such broad appeal is, that they express a theme people recognize in their own lives. The chord they strike resonates with their own longing. And the obstacles to achieving these goals are apparent everywhere: strife, resentment, anger, stubbornness, fear, insecurity, etc.

Yearning to be connected, wanting to belong, to be part of a larger reality, these are motives that turn up in everyone's life. Much of what you do is motivated by your inner drive to become or to stay connected to others. You spend time and energy to be with your family and relatives and to enjoy their company, because you want to be close to people who mean much to you. You offer your friendship to others to whom you feel a certain attraction, hoping to build on that so that you can truly share your life with a friend. You become a parent volunteer at school to encourage your own children, as well as express your concern and love for all children.

These are the positive examples. Many of the so called negative experiences in life result from this very same yearning, the yearning to love and to be loved, the yearning to be connected. Only here this yearning has somehow derailed. Unfortunately, this is an all too common experience in everyone's life. It can happen when people cling to something from the past, be it a relationship, an object or a habit. They continue loving a cherished memory instead of loving the present moment. Then when a new opportunity to come into contact with another person presents itself, they do not recognize it and let it pass. Insecurity, stubbornness or prejudice stand in the way of a new, unexpected experience. And its promise of building bridges to others will go unnoticed. Or the longing for love turns into the wish to recapture a piece of paradise thought lost. Insecurity and shyness prevent people from reaching out. Because of that they miss the next opportunity to connect, and a cycle of disappointment and frustration is set in motion. It happens to all of us. We become upset over another person's inability to live up to her or his potential, thereby missing the opportunity to offer encouragement.   Rejection often wins, where a hug could have accomplished so much.

Faith, hope and love, as well as struggle, strife and rejection; all are present in and around us. They express the urge to associate with an aspect of Creation, be it a person, a cause or ideal, or nature. It is the desire to be in connection with Spirit in any of its expressions.

FINE-TUNING THE COMPASS

The one spiritual ideal that we humans share with the entire creation is to be in connection with Creation (or God, Spirit, the Creative Forces, All, Love, or any other name you prefer). *Connection to the Creative Forces* or *Oneness with God* is the one universal ideal, the universal compass. It is very important that you can relate your individual ideal to the decisions and choices of your daily life. Therefore, you need to fine-tune the   universal compass such, that you can feel and see the intent right next to any circumstance in which you might find yourself. The one universal ideal *Oneness with God* needs narrowing down a bit to fit you. To this end you will choose one or two of the aspects in which oneness with God finds expression in the world, like Love, Hope, Beauty, Justice, Service, Cooperation, Intelligence. But these aspects in and of themselves still do not give you enough grip to work with when confronted with child related problem situations - you will need a working level spiritual ideal. Take your ideal and specify it further, making it more practical and enhancing its meaningfulness. For example:

Love	becomes	*Manifest God's love in the family*
Hope	becomes	*Motivator and helper,* or *Receptive listener*
Service	becomes	*Healer of bodies,* or *Assist as the Spirit directs*

You will discover and define your very own individual set of ideals, when you follow the sequence of exercises and questions, called *The Twelve Step System for the Setting of Ideals.* This system will guide you through the process of finding the intent that lies at the basis of your life. Then you will see how you can express your personal intent into new attitudes and actions regarding your relationship with your children. You will learn how to express who you really are in the middle of your everyday life shared with your kids. And you will discover the positive influence spiritual development can have on parenting and how being a parent can spur you on to grow as a person. For the following exercises you will need:

- A time slot in which you know you will not be disturbed or distracted
- A rested body, a quiet mind, and a sincere intent to learn about your life's truth
- A pencil and notebook, and a copy of the worksheet in the appendix if you like

Read this and the following chapter first, before actually doing the exercises. That will give you a general idea of the process and it might prevent wrong turns. Take your time when doing these exercises. When asked to write down your thoughts, put down anything that comes to mind. Sifting and selecting will come later. Do not feel embarrassed; nobody but yourself will ever see what you have written. The reason you need to write your answers down is so that you can compare your present thoughts to thoughts you write down at a future time, and see changes and new insights. In that way your development becomes apparent.

THE TWELVE STEP SYSTEM FOR THE SETTING OF IDEALS

Step 1 - Heroes

Are there, or have there been, people in your life you look up to, or people you consider heroes? Are there people you particularly admire because of a certain trait or accomplishment? They can be historical people, well-known people, family members, acquaintances, it does not matter. Write down the name of the first person that comes to mind. Behind the name specify why that person stands out for you. What are her/his particular attributes that you like? What do you admire about her/his accomplishments? Be very specific. Continue doing this for every person you want to include in your list. Again, be specific: Why and What. Examples:

Maria	for her <u>faith</u> and <u>dedication</u>
Mother Theresa	for her <u>service</u> and <u>renunciation of ego</u>
Beethoven	for his <u>dedication</u> to his art and <u>communication</u> beyond words
Granddad J.:	for his <u>savvy</u> and <u>"down to earth"-iness</u>

etc.

Underline each virtue or attribute of the people mentioned and list them separately. When you come upon a quality for a second (or third) time, simply put a check before the word. From the above example:

> *faith*

V *dedication*

> *service*

> *renunciation of ego*

> *communication, etc.*

Try to see if two qualities can actually be pulled into one. For example, if you consider *renunciation of ego* a form of *dedication*, then cross off that item and *dedication* receives a second check.   If you would rather group it under *service*, you could do that. It depends on how you define and how you feel about a certain quality.

Step 2 - Personal qualities

Write down eight to ten of your personal qualities such as talents, strengths, abilities, aptitudes, etc. Some of them you probably already put to use. Others you may not have used yet, but you   feel they are there. Here are a few examples to help you get started.   While reading through the list immediately mark the ones that appeal to you.

friendly	*energetic*
sensitive	*psychic*
empathetic	*decisive*
forgiving	*leadership*
patient	*wise*
cooperative	*sense of humor*
loyal	*listener*
innovative	*committed*
creative	*good with animals or ...*
imaginative	*good with hands or ...*
practical	*writing*
artistic	*cooking*
industrious	*teaching*
logical	*financially adept*
motivator	*mechanically skilled*
....	....

Step 3 - Weaknesses and faults

Now consider the following: Each of us has weaknesses and faults, that we do not like to dwell on. Consider the possibility that a   weakness can become a strength. Suppose a weakness like possessiveness or wanting to control another person's life, really is the back side of the coin called *being supportive* or *empathic*. Or quick irritation is the flip side to a *quest for quality*. Try to identify two to four personal weaknesses, and write these down. Examine each one and see if you can perceive a flip side quality to that particular weakness. At this point you probably will not find a positive quality for every single weakness you list, but add the ones you do discover to the list of personal qualities you made in step 2. And if already listed, put a check before the word.

Step 4 - Your parents' intentions

Consider your parents. For each in turn try to define your interpretation of what it is they stand (or stood) for in life. Suppose you think of your father as a gregarious person. Both at work and at home relationships and good communication are important to him. Even if his desire to be liked by other people irritates you, looking through this appearance you might see his intention to be in harmony with other people. Then from your perspective, your dad stands for *harmony*. Suppose you think of your mother as a helpful and caring person. At home and at work she is always ready to lend a helping hand, always concerned about other people's well being. Even if you feel her loving actions are strangling you, or that her inquiries about other people's lives make her a busy-body, you might still conclude that beneath all that slumbers the intention to care of others. Then, from your perspective, your mom stands for *caring*. Write down the intentions of your parents' lives. Then take the ones you feel also apply to your own life and add those to the list of step 2 (personal qualities). If already listed, put a check before the word.

Step 5 - Accomplishments

Make a list of accomplishments you have made during your life so far, and of every single one put down why you are proud of it. Examples:

accomplishment	why you are proud
As a 16 year old my team won the state youth soccer tournament	It shows <u>cooperation</u>, <u>dedication</u>, <u>expression of physical energy</u>
At 22 moved across US to start a new job	It shows <u>vision</u>, <u>courage</u>, <u>the will to pull up sleeves</u>
Stayed at sick mother's bedside through thick and thin	It shows <u>willingness to serve</u>; discovered <u>ability to encourage</u>

Underline the personal qualities you listed and put them on a separate list. Check to see if there are qualities that express more or less the same underlying virtue. For example, *physical energy* and *willingness to pull up sleeves* could both be captured under: *practical dedication.* So cross out both items and write down *practical dedication* with a check. Put a check for any item that comes up again.

Step 6 - Moments of self-actualization

Review your life for events or moments when you were deeply inspired and thought, or might have thought: "This is the real me coming through!" Think of moments when you felt vibrantly alive and happy. Also think of occurrences in your life when you felt that you played a key role and loved it. It might or might not have been a moment that changed your life. Other people might or might not have noticed that it happened. What we are after are moments when you had a strong sense of self-actualization. Take your time to think about this. Write down exactly what it is that occurred, what you were doing or thinking, and why the event impressed you.

After listing your stories of self-actualization you review them one by one. Is there a particular virtue of which the story speaks? Write that virtue down next to the story. If not, underline the key words in the story, and see if they point in the direction of a personal quality. Make a list of the personal qualities identified by this exercise (put checks where doubles occur). See if you can group two or more qualities together under one name (in that case do not forget to check the group name).

Step 7 - Merging lists

In this step you will merge the four lists of qualities you have made so far. Put before you on the table the list from step 1 (heroes), next to that the list from steps 2-4 (personal qualities) and step 5 (accomplishments), and next to that the list from step 6 (moments of self-actualization). Are there any qualities that occur on all four lists? Highlight those with a color marker.

Merge the four lists. Take the longest one as a basis, hold the second largest next to it and put a check before a word on the basis list every time it is mentioned on the second list. Add new qualities at the end of the basis list. Do the same with the two remaining lists.

Step 8 - Core group of personal qualities

Out of this new list you will attempt to find a core of four or five personal qualities that will help you in defining your working level spiritual ideal. Read through this final list and consider the various attributes. Consider the highlighted entries especially, as well as the ones with checks behind them. Which of these do you feel are very much a part of you? Some of them belong to the essence of your being and you cannot imagine yourself to be without them. Which ones call up the best in you? Underline the qualities you feel are at the basis of your being in this world.

As an aid in selecting your core group of personal qualities, place yourself in Life's shoes. Through which qualities would Life choose to express itself through you? All personal qualities have the potential of becoming God-qualities. Which ones come to mind if you think about it in this way? Maybe you want to add a potential quality to your core list; a quality that does not find expression at this moment yet, but could be expressed in the future.

At the completion of step 8 you should have a small list of four or five qualities that you feel represent the highest possible good in you.

Step 9 - Team

Think of your core qualities as a team. What is this team most suited to do or be? In what direction does this group point? Again, take your time to reflect. Let your pencil rest and close your eyes. When an idea pops into your mind, write it down. When ideas do not come, skip this step, and continue with the next one.

Step 10 - Finding your working level spiritual ideal

Consider a list of sample working level spiritual ideals. These are not descriptions of careers or jobs. They refer to the value behind what you do, as the following example shows:

Bill chooses for his ideal *To make life pure.* This intent points to the quality of purity to be at the basis of attitudes and actions in his life. He is committed to purity in motives and actions. This does not mean that Bill needs to start a career in the cleaning business, although that is not excluded either. Whatever the kind of work he is involved with, he will certainly find opportunities there to apply his ideal. His work place might or might not be the principal place where he expresses his spiritual ideal. He could express his ideal in a hobby or in volunteer work. Certainly in relation to his family he will be able to bring his intention of purity in motives and actions into manifestation. In fact, in almost any field of interest it is possible to find a way to express an ideal. You will see how, when we come to the mental and physical ideals in steps 11 and 12.

Now back to your working level spiritual ideal. When reading the following example ideals, stop and consider each one individually. Do you feel any affinity with it? Does it sound right for you? Does it reflect one or more of your core personal qualities that you identified earlier? Try to formulate a few sample ideals to add to the list. They do not necessarily have to reflect your position. The aim is to get practice in finding words for intents that come from the realm beyond words. Here are some examples of working level spiritual ideals to get you started:

To be an agent of peace and truth
To be an innovator
To be a healer of minds
To be a healer of bodies
To be a communicator and clarifier of ideas
To be a receptive listener
To be a worker for justice and peace
To cooperate with Spirit in nature
To be a catalyst for change and growth
To bring hope and joy to the desperate
To be a spiritual inspirer through .... (e.g., art, words)
To complete and perfect and make things whole
To care for the people around me
To appreciate and bring beauty
To discern and analyze life's questions
To be a celebrator and a channel of joy
To unify and make whole the fragments of life
To be an agent of justice and hope
To manifest God's Love in the family
To straighten the way for unobstructed   communication
To bring harmony and peace in my own world
To show compassion for those less fortunate
To awake faith
To bring hope and joy in service to my neighbor

Now comes the time to choose a tentative definition of your working level spiritual ideal. One or more of these examples might come close to what you feel your intent might be. You can adapt the words so they suit you, or define your own wording. Again, take your time with this most important step. Put down what you believe to be the   best possible representation of your innermost intent at the present time. It might help to write down several versions and   compare them.   You can settle for two or three candidate formulations and then come back to it tomorrow. After sleeping it over and looking at it from some distance, one of them will probably stand out for you.

Do not hesitate to play around with the wording. You might be surprised by the loftiness of your wording or by its simplicity. It does not matter how long or how short the sentence is, as long as you feel it captures the essence of your life as you are conscious of it now.   The wording you choose will not be set in stone. Over time you will probably want to adjust it so it reflects your intent at that later moment.

Step 11 - Finding your mental ideals

Defining your mental ideals is your next job. Mental ideals flow from and express your chosen spiritual ideal. They relate to the world of thoughts, attitudes, emotions, ideas, plans, resolves, beliefs, drives, outlook, etc. Going back to the example of the previous chapter, Carol's spiritual ideal *Guide children* was stretched out, so to speak, to the world of the mind. There it was translated into:

- *Practice patience and tolerance with my kids*

- *Be open to opportunities to work with groups of children*

- *Bring hope to the troubled teen next door*

She might have added to her mental ideals list *Nourish the child in other adults and in me.* And then, thinking of her relationship with her husband, she could resolve to find more ways to laugh and enjoy their time together.

Another person with different talents and interests might   choose different mental ideals flowing from the same spiritual ideal, e.g.:

- *Get more involved in my children's lives,* or

- *Gain knowledge in the field of pedagogy and children's psychology*

The point is to translate the spiritual ideal into a mental ideal that fits you, that makes you feel comfortable.

As this example shows you need to select a few areas, a few situations, on which to concentrate. For this purpose you can use the ideals targets provided in the appendix, or make your own. Take a blank piece of paper and draw a small circle in the center, just large enough to contain the words of your spiritual ideal. Write your ideal in the small circle.

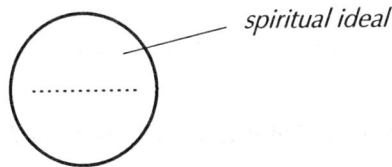

spiritual ideal

Fig. 1

Now draw a larger circle around it about twice the radius of the first. This section will contain your mental ideals. Draw two lines: from top to bottom and from side to side, skipping the inner circle.

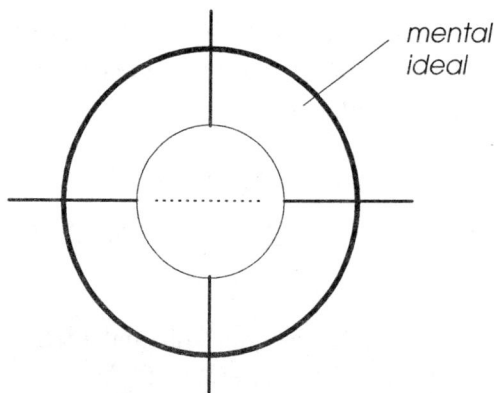

Fig. 2

Choose four areas you would like to work on. Since the parent-child relationship is the focal point in this book, it makes sense to put "children" in one of the four corners. Other possible areas are: spouse, relative, neighborhood, friend, workplace, colleague, church, hobby, career, self, etc. Write your other choices down in the three corners left. You can add more subjects later, in a new "target" if you like.

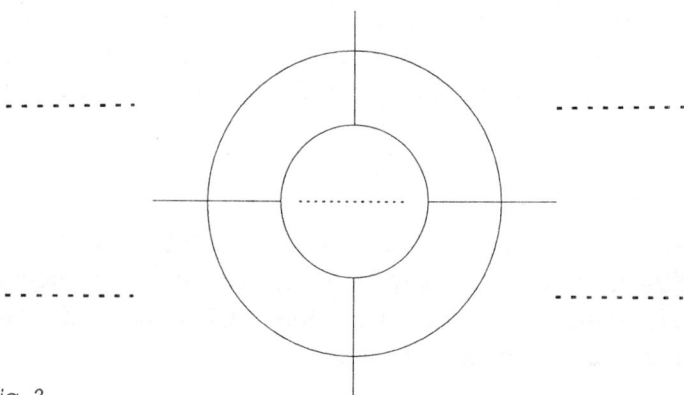

Fig. 3

Take your time to analyze each of the four chosen work areas, one at a time. For the first area ask yourself: "In the light of my stated spiritual ideal, what attitude, perspective or resolve would be the best to try out or adopt?" Try to be specific enough so you will have a tool to your disposal, but not too specific. You want to remain flexible and able to respond to situations freely.

By defining a mental ideal you consciously choose an intent that will guide you. It is something you can come back to when you are at your wit's end, or have no clue how to proceed. You will be able to analyze your own attitude and motivation in any concrete situation and tell whether or not you measured up to your stated mental ideal. An example might clarify this.

Let's consider Anita. She and her three year old daughter, Eve, have a close relationship. Anita is a devoted mother and Eve is as healthy and bubbly as a three year old could be. This morning, as usual, Eve does not accept the clothes her mother selects for her and flings them to the floor. The clothes Eve wants to wear are totally inappropriate, both for the time of year, as for the activities planned for the day. They are both upset and close to tears when Anita finally tries to force the clothes over Eve's head. Anita is ready to throw in the towel, right next to the pile of rejected clothes, when she stops and pauses. She decides to consider this recurring problem in the light of her framework of ideals. Her spiritual ideal is *To be a worker for justice and peace* and her mental ideals in the area of her children are *To be fair* and *To trust my inner guidance*. Anita comes to the conclusion that forcing Eve to wear her mother's choice of clothing is inconsistent with her spiritual ideal. She will not be tempted again to solve the problem this way. She looks for an alternative way to respond. She lets justice (from *To be a worker for justice*) and fairness (from *To be fair)* point the way. The bottom shelf of Eve's closet will be reserved for a small variety of clothing appropriate for the current season. Eve will choose her clothes from this shelf and dress herself. Whenever Anita is tempted to get emotionally involved in Eve's dressing herself she will, on cue, consult her inner guidance (as explained in Chapter 7.) She will make herself available as a channel of help, as opposed to becoming an opinionated parent. That way she will not encroach on Eve and the result for both of them will be peace. By changing both her attitude and her routine Anita has effectively applied her spiritual ideal *To be a worker for justice and peace.* She is able to express what she holds most dearly in her relationship with her daughter.

Now let's go back to your task of wording your own mental ideals. Make sure they do not contain the word "should." That word triggers the wrong associations. This is a voluntary effort, and self coercion is out of place and will backfire. Do not place your mental ideals too far removed from where you are right now. You should be able to imagine living up to its calling, at least some of the time. Limit yourself to one or two mental ideals per work area. Then, move on to the second segment, repeating the same process. Likewise for segments three and four.

Should you, at any point during this exercise, feel uncomfortable or forced, it might be that you need to rephrase your spiritual ideal. Refer to your four lists and see if perhaps you forgot to incorporate an important feature in the wording of your ideal. Try to play around with changing it so that the feature is represented. If still not satisfied, you might have to go back to earlier steps and compose new lists of features. Do not become discouraged. Where there is a will, there is a way. If you feel excited and are eager to go on, that is a sign you are on the right track.

Step 12 - Finding your physical ideals

Draw a third circle, as large as possible, around the second one. This new section will contain your physical ideals in the four chosen areas.

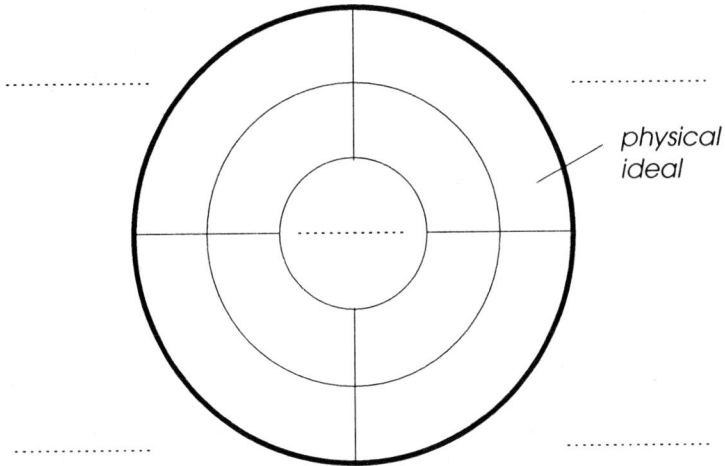

physical ideal

Fig. 4

The physical ideals will bring into manifestation your inner intent, that was captured by the wording of the spiritual ideal and made tangible by the defining of the mental ideals. Mental ideals, stretched out and translated into the world of action and matter, result in physical ideals. The physical ideals are intrinsically linked to both mental and spiritual ideals. They express, represent, reinforce and clarify the underlying inner motivation of your life.

It is important to remember that you are working with *intent* as opposed to outcome or *goals*. Physical *goals* refer to material conditions and things to own. Once achieved or obtained, you move on to the next goal. Physical *ideals*, however, have a more enduring quality since they refer to application and behavior that is a manifestation of what you know to be true in your heart. Examples:

Outcome oriented physical *goal*	**Intent oriented physical** *ideal*
Enroll child in art degree program	Encourage child to express self
Earn $60,000 a year	Provide a living
Buy a new car	Take care of transportation needs
Lose ten pounds	Act responsibly toward body
Get colleague A to stop looking over my shoulder	Communicate with A, find out what is bothering him

In the largest circle on your paper, in each work area, try to define what actions would follow logically from the stated mental ideals. In the example of Carol we see that she chose the following:

Area	Physical ideal
my children	- *Postpone dishes till after kid's bedtime*
	- *Stay focused on kids during bath time*
	- *At bedtime be firm about one story and one song per child*
church and school	- *Volunteer to set up a music program*
	- *Have kid's friends over for story and music time*
	- *Enlist to help with fundraising for local teen center*
neighborhood	- *Ask teen to help at home at modest pay*
	- *Ask teen if interested in preparations for teen center*

There are many other actions possible. Examples:

Area	Physical ideal
my children	- *Reserve time to help with homework*
	- *Gradually introduce them to house chores*
	- *Buy some kid size musical instruments and take time to play with them*
church/school	- *Ask teacher if help in the classroom is needed*
	- *Ask to be on the Sunday school curriculum committee*
teen neighbor	- *Invite teen along to baseball game*

Take your time to think of ways to express what you hold dearly. Again, if you are not sure, put down various alternatives, with or without question mark, and come back to it later. Also, refer back to your core group of personal qualities from step 8. Some of them are probably not directly represented in the statement of your spiritual ideal. This is the place to incorporate them consciously in your life to help make your life's intent manifest.

In the example of Carol we saw that her musical interest and ability already found an outlet in school and church. Suppose another talent of hers is that she is good with plants. She can incorporate that ability in her work with groups of children, e.g., *Organize vegetable patch on school campus,* or with drawing out the teen next door.

If you feel very uncomfortable and ideas do not come at all, then maybe the definitions of your mental ideals do not fit you. In that case, go back to the previous section and define your mental ideals over again. If it still does not feel right, refer to the section on finding the spiritual ideal. You may have taken a wrong turn. Do not feel bad or impatient, the work you are doing is well worth doing and very much worthy of your time. When you are on the right track you should feel energized and ready to go.

Limit the physical ideals to one, two or maybe three per work area.

Testing Your Ideals

So far, just words. Now comes the time of testing the compass, the time of trial and error. Stating ideals in and of itself does not bring growth. Application and experience do. It is possible that when you apply the physical ideal, you run into obstacles. Also, making wrong turns is part of this process. Should you go down a wrong track, do not become discouraged. This is not an examination, it is a discovery, and exploring new territory always brings with it tentative steps and wrong turns. Though you may get impatient, the upside is that you get to know the territory. And when you do find your direction you will be sure it is right, because you can compare.

To begin with, choose to work with two or three of the physical ideals you wrote down. Pick the ones you think will yield a measurable result. Do not try the hardest ones yet. When doing your "assignment" look for signs that show you are on the right track. After applying your physical ideals for a period of time you can experience any or all of the following signs:

Joy. You will start to feel joyous, not only when engaged in the activity, but at other times as well.

Purpose. You will start to sense what your purpose is here on earth. You will develop a sensitivity for the singleness of purpose in the world and life around you. Of course that will contribute to the feeling of joy.

Wholeness. You will feel your life coming together, not fragmented any longer. You have allowed your spiritual, mental and physical aspects to become integrated, at least partly. The framework of ideals is providing you with a means to lift up your life as a whole.

Wonder. You will start to feel life's presence around you, expressing in all kinds of creatures, forms and situations. You will gain, if you do not have that already, an appreciation for the quality of life present in nature.

Positive influence on others, either directly by helping them, or indirectly by being a wholesome, joyous person who radiates love and hope (and, as you may know, these things are contagious). Appreciation can come to you directly, but it can also come indirectly, when you notice the positive impact your new action has on another person.

There are two kinds of applications: an activity or expressed attitude that requires just you to change, and an activity where you enter an existing situation.

With the first kind you can test and experiment and rely solely on your own judgment to decide whether this change is a success or not. An example is Carol's decision to postpone dishes till after the kid's bedtime. It is up to Carol to analyze the effects of her new action. It is up to her to decide if she wants to stop, change or continue with it.

With the second kind, the application within an existing situation, you will have to be sensitive to the way your new activity fits into it and is being received by others. Suppose you have chosen an activity that measures up to your chosen ideals. But when you actually engage in it, it somehow does not feel on target. In some cases that is a sign that you are not on the right track. The test indicates that this is not what you need to be doing. But it could also mean that you need to redesign the proposed action somewhat. Maybe a slight change of focus will set you straight.

Consider Carol's case. At her church she volunteered to start a music class for preschoolers on Sunday afternoons. It appears that another church member has already put together a program for kids ages 3 to 6 with various art and music activities, and at this moment there is no need for another program. Carol could decide she will try her luck at her children's school. Or she could decide to keep her physical ideal flexible and contact the person in charge of the existing program, to see if she needs any help, musical or otherwise.

Carol's next door neighbor, the teen in trouble, does not appreciate her suggestions at all. He is downright hostile. She does not want to force herself on another person. So, what is she to do? At some later time she could try again and suggest some shared activity, or she could talk to the teen's parents. Maybe they need someone who listens to their story more than the teen does. On the other hand, the whole matter might just not feel right for Carol to become involved in, and she decides to cross off this item on her physical ideals list.

This brings us to another point. It is possible that when you analyze your life and your activities, you have to conclude that one or more of them do not rhyme with your chosen spiritual ideal. Basically there are three options:

— Continue with the activity

— Stop the activity if possible, and look for a way to spend your time and energy in a way that is more in tune with your ideal

— Try to express your ideal in the activity

Let's look at the example of Carol once more. She works part time as a receptionist at the office of a newspaper.

Now that she is aware of the intent that is operative in her life (*Guide children*) she is eager to express it. Although her work is not her "first love", she does not dislike it either, and the money earned is very welcome. For now, she could decide to continue with the activity, but not to include her work in her target of ideals.

The second option, to stop the activity, would mean to quit her job. She believes that that would be too drastic a thing to do at this point in time. Instead, she could start to actively look for similar work in a child related setting (e.g., doctor's office, school, etc.)

The third option would be to take one or more of her mental ideals and try to express it in her current work place. *Practice tolerance and patience* can clearly be manifested at a reception desk. After a trial period, Carol could very well decide that her work place has become an area of application of ideals.

When you analyze your life, you might come upon an attitude or a habit that is not in tune with your spiritual and/or mental ideals. Unfortunately, old habits die hard, as do attitudes. In situations like this it helps to have a clear view of your ideals and what they mean to you. Your ideals can inspire you to come up with an alternative way of responding to people and situations. You can prepare yourself ahead of time with a clear image of the new attitude that naturally flows from your spiritual ideal. Then you will be alert to the moment when you can choose to behave in a different way, and you are no longer victim of circumstance or habit. In moments like these an affirmation can help you remember what you are about, as the following example shows.

Anita, mentioned earlier, let her framework of ideals lead her to a new way to deal with dressing her daughter

Eve in the morning. She decided to let Eve choose her own outfit from a small variety of options. Clothes and styles matter to Anita. She always chooses her own clothing with care and she has distinctive taste. Of course, her three year old daughter cannot match her level of sophistication, and Anita has a hard time holding back her suggestions and criticism. However, Anita is determined to live her ideals and she devises an affirmation for each time she is on the verge of remarking on Eve's way of dressing. She mentally steps out of the situation for a moment and says to herself:

I love your eyes, I love your smile
Those are all I need right now

Then she waits until she has thought of something nice to say to Eve. Anita's determination to live her ideals has led her to a new way to respond to a recurring troubling situation. One that recognizes and respects her own as well as her daughter's feelings.

An affirmation, like the one from this example, can prove to be a very effective tool to use when you feel that the interaction between you and your child is heading in the wrong direction. In Chapter 6 you will learn how to make an affirmation and how to use it.

A compass on a ship can only prove its worth when the captain consults it regularly. Then, when a hurricane hits, he knows how to stay on course. It works the same way with spiritual ideals. The stormy waters of parenting demand a stable instrument to set the course and stay with it. To work with a spiritual ideal is to live it day by day. By living it day by day, you connect your thoughts with your deeds, you connect your   heart with your hands.

Your intent shines through in what you do. Living your individual Spiritual ideal forges who you are with what you do.

APPLICATION

Now that you have read the entire chapter, you are ready to work with the *Twelve Step System for the Setting of Ideals*. If you cannot readily see where this business of setting ideals fits into parenting as you know it, you might want to read through the next chapter first.

Remember to take your time with each step. Do not force yourself to invent an answer. If ideas do not come naturally, put the book aside and let it rest for a while. The whole idea is to work with input that represents who you really are.

Also, do not hesitate to come back to an answer later, and change it. This is not a "right or wrong" kind of exercise. This is a process of becoming aware of themes and motives. Crossing out and redefining are all part of that process.

3

PARENTING AND IDEALS

You are the bows from which your children as
living arrows are sent forth

Kahlil Gibran

WHY DID YOU BECOME A PARENT?

Usually people do not ask themselves this question.
They might ask: "Why do I want to have children?"
And their answers vary. But no one asks beforehand why
he or she wants to become a parent. I know of only one
parent who was aware that what she wanted was as much
to be a mother as to have a child. It is really quite naive if
you think about it. It is almost as if you want to have the
White House without ever considering that that would
mean you would have to become the president of the
United States. This is not a coincidental comparison.
Different in scope and detail as these two occupations,
being a parent and being the president, may be, they are
surprisingly similar. They are alike in terms of the
constancy of demands as well as the potential to transform
a person. Both are "100%-kind-of-jobs." You either

commit to it for the full 100% of your being, or you should not take it on.

The size of the commitment and the length of time you are actively involved in parenting certainly warrant a clear vision of yourself as a parent. What expectations do you have of yourself and of your life, now that you are a parent? It is interesting to reflect on these questions and see if you can come up with some suggestions or answers.

Kahlil Gibran, in his timeless book "The Prophet," beautifully describes his vision of parents and children:

> *"And a woman who held a babe against her bosom said,*
> *Speak to us of Children.*
> *And he said:*
> *Your children are not your children.*
> *They are the sons and daughters of Life's longing for itself.*
> *They come through you but not from you,*
> *And though they are with you, yet they belong not to you.*
> *You may give them your love but not your thoughts.*
> *For they have their own thoughts.*
> *You may house their bodies but not their souls,*
> *For their souls dwell in the house of tomorrow, which you*
> *cannot visit, not even in your dreams.*
> *You may strive to be like them, but seek not to make them*
> *like you.*
> *For life goes not backward nor tarries with yesterday.*
> *You are the bows from which your children as living*
> *arrows are sent forth.*
> *The archer sees the mark upon the path of the infinite, and*
> *He bends you with His might that His arrows may go swift*
> *and far.*

Let your bending in the archer's hand be for gladness;
For even as he loves the arrow that flies, so He loves also
the bow that is stable."

Kahlil Gibran, "The Prophet"

DOES PARENTING FIT INTO YOUR LIFE?

From their first cry to their high school graduation parties and   beyond, your children's lives   are closely intertwined with your   own.   From now on till   you die (and   beyond!) you and   your children are   intensely connected.   What your   children do, how   they behave and react, and what they accomplish,   will affect   you deeply. Living in   harmony with your children, now   as well   as when   they are   adults themselves,   is one   of life's blessings.

Parents can   do a great deal to work toward   a harmonious relationship with their children,   in terms of respect, dedication and shared activities, to name just a few.   That, in and of   itself, is enough   reason to   consider parenting   a life's   task, worthy   of your sincere dedication and effort.

Now let us consider the   children.   If the parents cannot really fit guiding   and dedication into   their lives, what   kind of guidance and dedication do the children receive?   They will have   to make   do with the crumbs that   fall off the   table.   On   the other hand, if the parents clearly see   that rearing their children   is part of their individual plan   for life,   the children's   circumstances change dramatically.   On   account of the children   it is very important that parenting   fits into the   parents' life path. So the question "Does parenting fit into my life?" becomes

"*How* does parenting fit into my life?" The answer to this question lies in your spiritual ideal. When you express your innermost intent in the contact with your children, you will see how parenting is a part of your life plan.

HOW TO EXPRESS IDEALS IN THE PARENT-CHILD RELATIONSHIP

In the previous chapter you followed the stepwise method to become aware of your individual life theme, your spiritual ideal. You also identified the attitudes and perspectives that naturally flow from your spiritual ideal. Next you devised practical actions and changes that express the underlying spirit. This chapter deals with the application of ideals specifically in the parent-child relationship.

Even when your spiritual ideal does not explicitly point into the direction of children (as does *Guide Children*), a way can be found to express and apply it in your interaction with them. Let's look at some examples that will show you how you too can apply your spiritual ideal in the contact with your children. They will help you get started to think in terms of applied ideals. Each example makes clear how the inner motivation that lies at the basis inspired the physical applications. Parenting becomes a source of joy and discovery when, through your daily activities, you can express who you truly are.

To be an innovator

Suppose your spiritual ideal is *To be an innovator* and you successfully identify various physical ideals regarding your career and say, for instance, your involvement with a yacht club.   Now you need to find a way to express what you hold dearly (innovating) in the relationship with your children. One way is to actively involve them in your new activities at the yacht club. By consciously making them part of your projects they will sense your dedication and fire for solving things in original, new ways, and thus you inspire them. Apart from that though, you do not clearly see a way to connect your ideal with your children.

When that happens there is another way open to you. Take some freedom with the mental ideals and let them be inspired not only by your chosen spiritual ideal but by some other intent as well. Look at your core group of personal qualities (Chapter 2, step 8). Consider which one(s) you want to use in your contact with your children, together with your innovating spirit. Suppose *humor*, or *clarity* is in your core group. *Humor* combined with *innovation* can produce some nice possibilities:

spiritual ideal:	*- To be an innovator*
mental ideal, combined with *humor*:	*- Make time to have fun together*
physical ideal:	*- To set up clown's act with child to perform at family reunion, fair, or hospital*

Reflect on the physical ideal *To set up a clown's act with your child.* You could do this to show off your originality, or to please relatives. But when you do it to share with your child of your life's essence, in this case humor and laughter, it becomes a truly meaningful activity, both to you and your child.

When the spiritual ideal *To be an innovator* is combined with *clarity* it becomes a little harder to find a concrete way to manifest that intent in the contact with your children. However, your innovative spirit will surely find a manner to put *clarity* to good use, e.g.,

spiritual ideal:	*- To be an innovator*
mental ideal, combined with *clarity*:	*- Reach for clarity in motives and in communication*
physical ideal:	*- Guide child in verbal expression and explanation of feelings*

Even when it is hard to find a way to apply what you hold dearly in the contact with your children, it is important that you try. Because, as explained before, your child's experiences will affect you deeply.

To be an agent for peace and truth

The reason you include *peace* in the wording of your ideal is, that you love that quality in other people as well as in nature. You feel that to be at peace with yourself as well as with others and with your environment is absolutely essential if any kind of creative development is to happen.

The qualities of *peace* and *truth* both point toward inner life. They are found within. *Truth* appeals to you because you feel it is a condition for being at peace. *Truth* reminds you of honesty, clarity and sincerity, all features you admire and are eager to express, starting in the family. With these thoughts in the back of your mind, you decide to translate your spiritual ideal into the following mental ideals regarding your children:

spiritual ideal: - *Be an agent of peace and truth*

mental ideals: - *Experience nature*

- *Introduce children to prayer and meditation*

- *Be open about feelings and parental guidelines*

Now comes the practical application, namely the physical ideals. If you like biking, you could take your kids on a trip through a nature park. If you prefer sand and sea, why not take them to the ocean or to a lake. Nature exudes peace. Any place and any time you connect with it, the peace found in nature will carry over on you and your children.

To let your children experience inner life you encourage them to find words for their prayer. Openness about feelings and guidelines in practical terms means that you aim to keep the communication channels in the family open. Thus the following physical ideals result:

- *Make an effort to spend time together regularly in natural settings* (peace)

- *Involve kids in choosing time and wording of prayer* (peace and truth)

- *Explain motives; answer all questions; always hear child out* (truth)

These physical ideals, mundane and insignificant as they may seem, form the bridge that crosses the distance between your innermost intent (*peace* and *truth*) and your everyday life shared with your children.

To be an agent of justice and hope

Even as a child Becky remembers her keen sense for fairness. She would rebel when she felt that adults did not treat her or another child fairly. This same feature let her to study law and take up the profession of an attorney. She loves her work and is very dedicated. When considering her children she first looks for a way to express this same feature, love of *justice*, in her relationship with them. She feels that honesty really is a prerequisite for justice; if you are not honest about your own motives it becomes impossible to detect injustice and make improvements. So Becky decides to call her mental ideal *To be fair and honest*. She now considers steps she can take to express this ideal herself towards her kids, as well as steps that encourage them to be fair and honest. She decides to *Communicate and talk openly about own motives* and *Study conflict resolving techniques that involve children's input*, which now have become her physical ideals.

Next, to express her spiritual intent of *Hope* she feels that *To encourage* would be the right way to describe her mental ideal. She then thinks about ways to connect her world with her children's world. They participate in after school organized sports and Becky wants to make a link there. She decides *To be involved and watch her children's sport activities*. To summarize this process you can see that in Becky's case:

Justice led to	*fairness and honesty*, which led to	*- Communicate and talk openly about own motives* and
		- Study conflict resolving techniques that involve children's input
Hope led to	*encouragement*, which led to	*- involvement with children's sport activities*

Many parents watch their children's sports. But Becky's presence at games is different. Her involvement is directly connected to her awareness of her purpose in life. She is not there out of boredom, out of guilt or out of regret for her own missed opportunities. No, she is present because she wants to *encourage* (give *hope* to) her children with the things that matter to them. Through that motivation her presence gets a whole new meaning both to herself and to her kids.

To straighten the way for unobstructed communication

Laura is a to the point, no frills kind of person. She does not beat around the bush, and although it gets her into trouble at times, her directness is appreciated by many. She is an artist and her paintings carry this same quality. Thinking of her spiritual ideal *To straighten the way for unobstructed communication* in relation to her child, she feels that to keep the communication channels open the only possible attitude is *To let bygones be bygones*. She resolves to put this attitude into practice by using an affirmation when she or her child has become upset with the other.

To help her remember who she is and what she is about, she says quietly to herself:

> *You are life, and I am Life*
> *Life will freely flow when I will let it go*

Another of Laura's objectives is to link her life as an artist with that of her child who shows an interest in art. The word *accessibility* (her mental ideal) to her describes the motive to bring *unobstructed communication* into expression. She makes plans to do the following (her physical ideals):

- *Involve her child in one of her own projects*

- *Provide her child with her own corner and easily accessible art material*

- *Enroll her in drama or art class*

These actions are not really dramatic. Some children will ask for some of these things, or parents may decide they fit into a well-rounded education. But when Laura makes a conscious choice to let her child experience inspiration and communication through art, these activities suddenly receive a new dimension.

To be a communicator and clarifier of ideas

Vance heads his own company as a management consultant. Businesses seek his advice and suggestions on various aspects of business management, ranging from production optimization to restructuring. He is knowledgeable and quite successful in his work, which takes him all over the state. Consequently he is away from home often and even when in town, he makes long days at the office. Nevertheless, he is determined to manifest his inner intent, which clearly finds expression in his work, in the relationship with his 10 and 12 year old sons. On the basis of his spiritual ideal *To be a communicator and clarifier of ideas* he designs the following diagram, in keeping with his ability to clearly communicate ideas:

Acknowledge kids' viewpoint at all times on all subjects
(communicate)

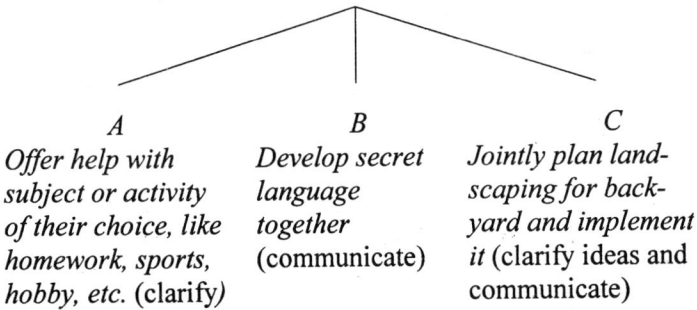

A	B	C
Offer help with subject or activity of their choice, like homework, sports, hobby, etc. (clarify)	*Develop secret language together* (communicate)	*Jointly plan land-scaping for back-yard and implement it* (clarify ideas and communicate)

Even if Vance does not spend much time with his children, the time they are together is very rewarding for all. He is open to his children's needs and wishes. And when helping them or working together he is able to do it in a way that fits him.

To be a healer of bodies

Lynn is a physician. She is in awe of the workings of the physical body. She finds it fascinating to discover the way in which the various bodily systems cooperate, and she is intrigued by the ability of the body to recuperate and heal itself. Clearly her profession is a primary area in which she connects the intent of her life with the work of her hands.

As you can see, this spiritual ideal is rather specific and not necessarily child-related. To connect her inner intent with her attitude towards her children, Lynn takes her lead from her overall perspective on life. She describes that as the desire *To respect and nurture creation in its various forms.* This perspective does not so much flow from her spiritual ideal to be a healer, as it is a related attitude, supporting her spiritual ideal of being a healer. It could also be seen as a spiritual ideal in its own right. She decides to develop decisions and actions relating to her children based on this perspective. She lets her *love of nature and a healthy, active body* (mental ideal) inspire her. And thus the following physical ideals result:

- *Take children camping to let them be with nature*

- *Practice favorite sport and encourage*
  children to become active in sports

Lynn cannot directly translate her life calling *To be a healer of bodies* into objectives relating to her kids. But she identifies a related intent that means just as much to her. This related intent inspires her to look for practical steps that express who she is in family relationships.

To be a healer of minds

Suppose you too are called to heal, like Lynn in the above example. Your focus, though, is on mental well being. You can express your calling through various professions, like therapist, teacher, group facilitator or social worker. You feel that *To keep a centered and open mind* is essential to do your work well. It is a related attitude that supports your spiritual ideal. When defining your ideals relating to your children, rather than choosing your life calling (*To be a healer of minds*) to guide you, you choose this related attitude as an inspiration (your mental ideal). Moreover, you and your family are animal lovers. Two dogs, several cats and a rabbit are part of your household. To you, caring for animals and being with them is not just enjoyable, it is therapeutic. It helps to center the mind. Consequently, the physical ideals you come up with, are:

- *Let kids "talk back" and hear them out*

- *Take time to enjoy pets together*

- *Volunteer at local zoo together*

The common theme of your framework of ideals is *To keep a centered and open mind*, which is essential to express your life calling, namely *To be a healer of minds*. It also finds specific expression, partly through animal related activities, in the contact with your children.

To be a catalyst for change and growth

Before she started her family Nancy used to work as a sales representative for a company in medical supplies. She loved the fast pace of her work and her contacts in the various sectors of health care. She also liked working in a team with people from other departments of her company to meet consumer needs and improve the quality of their products. Now Nancy is wife and mother of four, and she no longer works as a sales rep. Occasionally she helps out with special promotions and exhibitions. How can Nancy be a catalyst for change and growth in family life? She notices with amusement that the coming of her four children in and of itself is a testimony to her inner intent of change and growth! She strongly feels that change and growth are rhythmic. Preparation and gestation alternate

61

with expression and creation. She believes that vision, encouragement and patience lie at the basis of this rhythmic play. She decides to include the last two in her mental ideal, which becomes *To encourage and be patient*. From experience she knows that it is a lot easier to be patient with someone if you really understand that person. When you see the world with the other person's eyes, patience is almost easy to come by. So her first physical ideal is *To enter my children's world in thought* (meaning: listening) *and in deed* (meaning: take part in their activities, and play the part they want mom to play, sit in their chairs to really see the world through their eyes).

As far as encouragement is concerned Nancy feels that she already practices that ideal. But to improve on it she decides to try to be supportive and encouraging also in moments that it does not come to her naturally, namely when she is tired. She devises an affirmation to use when needed, to help her remember what her ideal is and what her children mean to her. When a child comes to her for support at a time when she is at the end of her rope, she says silently to herself:

You are a child of Life, and so am I
Show me what you really need and Life will stand by

Thus her framework of ideals has become:

spiritual ideal	*- Be catalyst for change and growth*
mental ideal	*- To encourage and be patient*
physical ideals	*- Enter their world in thought and deed* *- When tired use affirmation to encourage and support*

THE FLEXIBLE FRAMEWORK OF IDEALS

The framework of ideals is not a rigid system. Where one spiritual ideal will lend itself easily to be translated into mental and physical terms regarding any aspect of your life, another spiritual ideal will be applicable in only a limited way. If that is the case, look for supporting, underlying or related motives and perspectives. Your core group of personal qualities (Chapter 2, step 8) will point the way.

The boundaries between the ideals within the framework are not strict either. For instance, to one person the ideal *To show compassion for those less fortunate*, could feel so specific as to be a physical ideal. To a different person the same ideal feels more like a basic intent, inviting a spectrum of ideals relating to various subjects. It all depends on your point of view, your situation and your style. Do what feels right for you. And remember, it is the *underlying motivation* that makes your activities stand out.

Consider the analogy of a well-proportioned building, like a community center or a church, that has large windows all around. When night falls the windows light up. The structure and shape of the building recede in the dark. The rectangular windows cast out their bright white light. Now consider the same building after remodeling. Just like before, when night falls the windows light up. Only this time brightly colored designs of stained glass windows are revealed. Although inside the same white light is on, now, through the varied design of color and shape, it carries the quality of radiant beauty and warmth. You are like that building. When you open your inner door to let the Creative Forces flow through you, you illuminate the darkness around you. Then, when you consciously choose to express your spiritual ideal, your daily activities form the lead patterns that delineate the richly colored facets of your radiance.

Living with your children can be a joyful, enriching experience when you are consciously connected on three levels. Physically, by living together and sharing activities. Mentally, through encouragement, guidance and planning. And spiritually, by loving your children and sharing with them your life's deepest truth: your spiritual ideal. It is the intent that links the spiritual reality with the physical reality. When sincere intent manifests in the physical world, you are on your way to wholeness.

APPLICATION

The concept of linking intent with attitude and action is not as farfetched or remote as you may think. By reading this book you show your willingness to examine your role as a parent and the influence you have on your children's development. No doubt you have already become aware of the intent, of the underlying motivation of much of what you say and do regarding your children. The following questions will help you to become aware of how much you have already integrated intent with attitude and action. This awareness will assist you in discovering new ways to express your true self in the relationship with our children.

1. Think of an *action* or an *activity* you already share with your child in which you can recognize an underlying *intent* of which you might or might not have been aware. Examples:

    –   In the fall you and your child go out to the woods to search for mushrooms. You clean, chop and fry them together, and the whole family enjoys eating them - Sharing your Love of nature.

    –   You drive your child to school in the morning - This could be just routine or duty. But it could also be the expression of your commitment to your child's well being, and the expression of your joy to spend time together.

2. Think of an area in the relationship with your child where you can identify an *attitude* that is already inspired by an *intent* that lies beyond it. Examples:

   – Although you feel like hugging and praising your child when she is contentedly engaged in her play, you do not interrupt her out of respect of her privacy and the integrity of her play. You save your praise for later - Respect inspired by the intent to facilitate growth.

   – You deliberately put aside what you are doing and take time to really listen to your child attentively when she tells you about her day - Accessibility inspired by the intent to encourage.

Even if you have not yet devoted a section of your target of ideals to the area "own children," these exercises enable you to feel the connection you have already established between your innermost intent and practical day to day life with your kids. This new perspective can become a conscious way of life if you devote a section of the ideals target to your children, or to issues facing you both.

4

SPIRITUAL LIFE

And if you would know God be not therefore a
solver of riddles. Rather look about you and you
shall see Him playing with your children

Kahlil Gibran

In Chapter 1 you learned about the concept of three
levels of reality, namely the physical, the mental and the
spiritual reality. You then took the steps to custom make
your compass and fine-tune it. You learned how to link
your inner intent to attitudes and actions regarding your
children and yourself. You were able to see the ways in
which you can apply spiritual concepts in daily life with
kids, using the tool of the framework of ideals. Now is the
time to look at inner life.

This chapter and the following three chapters are about
inner life. By exploring inner life and through reflection
and contemplation you will get to know the spiritual world
and how it operates. You will discover the principles that
govern the spiritual world. To know about these principles
is as important to you as knowledge of the principles of
electricity is to a technician. A growing understanding of

the spiritual world will allow you to use the tool of the framework of ideals in daily life more and more effectively. Moreover, the next chapters will present several new tools as well. But before you read about these new instruments it is necessary to learn more about the Spirit and the spiritual world.

WHAT IS SPIRIT?

You may wonder what Spirit is, or who Spirit is. People use all kinds of words to describe it, like Universal Consciousness, Christ Consciousness, Life, Love, Father-Mother-God, Creative Forces, All, God, Brahma, Shakti, Tao, Wakonda, etc. The reason we cannot agree on one universal name, is perhaps because we cannot pin down what or who "it" is. In this respect it is interesting to learn what Kahlil Gibran writes about God:

> *"And if you would know God be not therefore a solver of riddles.*
> *Rather look about you and you shall see Him playing with your children.*
> *And look into space; you shall see Him walking in the cloud, outstretching His arms in the lightning and descending in rain.*
> *Your shall see Him smiling in flowers, then rising and waving His hands in trees."*

"The Prophet", by Kahlil Gibran

Yet, according to M. Scott Peck, God exists in the unconscious, ready and waiting for expression in consciousness ("The Road Less Traveled".) Apparently, "it" is without as well as within.

In the Bible God himself answers the question "who are you?" with: "I am that I am." That is a very puzzling reply. That little sentence eludes the reasoning mind. It could mean: "I am so that I can be." But it could also point to something different: "I am that particular I-am," referring to the one who is presently reading the answer: you! Thus it would mean: "I am who you are."

Various metaphysical writings point out that trying to capture God in a word or a sentence is futile. God, Spirit, is always more. It is vaster than human comprehension, so no wording flowing from human understanding can do it justice. It is the same with trying to define what music really is. If you can capture the essence of music with words, there is no need to express yourself in music. This analogy gives an idea of how limited words are. They serve us well in many areas, but the message is never found in the words but always beyond them. To explain it in musical terms: the music is everywhere but on the music sheet.

This inherent restriction of the expression through words is probably why Jesus so often told stories, or parables. People get hung up on a quote, as they still do today. With a story you cannot focus on a single line, on a sound bite. You have to soak up the entire story, and try to fathom its meaning and sense the quality of the underlying value.

Likewise with spiritual reality. You need to look beyond the words describing it. Try to look at this question from a different angle. In everyone's life, as no doubt in yours, there are or have been people who possess a measure of love and wisdom that makes them stand out over others. The quality of their life, the depth and quality of their empathy imbues you with a confidence that makes your walk seem lighter. Can you think of someone like that in your life's experience? To begin to get a feel for what Spirit is, think of the value this person represents to you. Try to imagine God, or Spirit expressing itself, among many ways, not only through a person or a thing, but as a "value of being." Where you cannot know God with words, you come a little closer by using your creative imagination. When Jesus talks about God he uses the words Abba (dad) and "Our Father." He points to the value behind the words dad and father.

It is legitimate to want to know what or who God or Spirit is and to expect an answer. It is understandable that you try to figure out what it is that pulls you and directs you. That does not mean that when you receive an answer you will recognize it right away or understand the full meaning instantaneously. Introspection, pondering and reflection are absolutely necessary, as are an open mind, a tenacity bordering on stubbornness, and a willingness to gain new perspectives that will topple familiar assumptions. And yet again: "... if you would know God be not therefore a solver of riddles. Rather look about you ..." (Kahlil Gibran).

It is a process, a process of listening and being led. You will understand the answers in small portions, a little bit at a time. The insights that come your way will be hard to put into words, because they come from a realm beyond the realm of words. Still, they will reveal themselves to be truth from beyond the mental and physical worlds.

Every single soul needs to experience anew the answer to the question "What is Spirit?" How can Spirit reveal itself to you? You cannot take it or buy it, you can only hold out your hands expectantly and receive it.

You express within yourself a desire to learn about the Spirit and try to prepare a place for it to enter, and then you wait. This is called turning within. Turning within is essential if you are determined and committed to learn about spiritual life. Take the time and effort to clear your mind of "worldly rubble". Ponder this issue about God (Spirit) and what it means in your life. Then experience that little by little the veil lifts. A new understanding dawns within, the truth will start to unfold. Ask and keep on asking, knock and keep on knocking. The sincere intent combined with the commitment to apply what you know so far, are what counts.

Living the life of a parent of small children is a great opportunity to learn about the ways in which Spirit expresses itself. It allows you to experience first hand Love and Joy and Hope. It is a perfect school to learn Patience and Gentleness and Self-control.

ENTERING SPIRITUAL REALITY

Even though your concept of what Spirit is may be vague or hard to describe, this should not keep you from experiencing the world of Spirit. When walking the spiritual path it is very helpful to have an idea of the characteristics of the terrain you are about to tread. All the questions you might ask in preparation for a trip to an unknown foreign country are justified questions to ask when entering the world of the Spirit. What does the landscape look like, how are the roads marked, how will I know that I am going the right way, what kind of food do the people eat, etc. If you want to hear the language, feel the ambiance and enjoy the scenery of a new land, you cannot stay at home and leaf through brochures. No, you need to cross the border and walk its paths.

Love, Light, Oneness, Wholeness, Truth, ... These key words start the list of features of spiritual reality. This list continues with more characteristics that are connected to or are aspects of these basic ones: kindness, compassion, understanding, perfection, harmony, health, peace, etc. Will you experience all these blessings when you cross the border line? Eventually, yes. However, when coming to a foreign country you need time to learn the language and time to learn the ways and customs before you can fully experience that life is different there. So here. In the measure that you learn to express the spiritual elements and make them part of your consciousness, do you experience their presence. In as much as you possess the spiritual features will they be reflected back to you. When you are loving, you will find love; when you are kind, you will meet kindness; when you are forgiving, you will become whole; when you give hope, you will see the light.

And through this all runs the thread of your intent to connect with your inner being, with your Source. In a way, the sincerity of your intent is the passport that gives you entry to any and all of the spiritual blessings. Without this passport you do not notice the landscape, you do not hear the language being spoken, you cannot even cross the border. The sincere intent relates to your desire to learn about life, to learn the truth, to be open to new insights. This means you have to let go of familiar assumptions and comfortable beliefs. You need to leave behind your personal blueprint of what life is.

You carry the passport of sincere intent on your heart as you start walking the path of the spiritual world.

In the order in which they are presented   you   try   to
incorporate   into   your   being   the various characteristics
of this world. As a result you will experience the beauty
of the landscape, the beauty of Creation: Oneness,
Wholeness, Perfection, Love, Light and more.

As you may expect, this does not happen automatically.
There is work involved. And work can hurt. You will need
to work with fragments and live through disharmony to
reach Oneness. The challenge is to let the bits and pieces
pass through your hands and forge them into One. Only
then can Oneness become a part of your being. It is the
same with the other features. In as much as you have
dedicated yourself to a certain feature and have
transformed its opposites through hard work, do you
possess that feature. And in the measure that you possess it
will it be reflected back to you.

SPIRITUAL PRINCIPLES

The physical world operates according to physical
principles that humankind has been able to identify over
the ages: the laws of gravity, electromagnetism, aero-
dynamics, etc. The workings of the physical world are not
left to chance. We know what will happen beforehand, we
recognize it when it happens and we can explain what has
happened afterwards.

Family life offers a nice example of experiencing this
predictability of a physical process. A toddler who is busy
throwing objects from the highchair is exploring a basic
physical principle: the law of gravity.   The toddler is
enthralled and delighted by   the   predictability   and
reliability of   the experiment.   Throw, wait,   BANG!
throw, wait, BANG! Over and over again.   Through

experience the toddler gets to know his world. The toddler does not need a formula or an explanation. Simply the repetition of: throw, wait, BANG!, allows the principle to become part of his experience, part of his life.

The mental world has principles as well. The mental principles have not been defined accurately as yet, nor have they been captured in neat formulas like the physical principles. Nonetheless, you use these principles in your life every day. When you encourage your child, he is more likely to enjoy and excel at an activity than when you criticize him. Your child is likely to repeat behavior that is rewarded. The human variation of the "Pavlov reflex" happens all the time. People have programmed themselves in thoughts and communications, or have let themselves be programmed, to respond predictably to certain cues. The way they respond depends on factors such as personality, upbringing, and culture. Often this programming is very helpful; it frees up mind space to think about other matters while performing a routine task. Driving a car is such a routine task. While you maneuver through traffic your mind may be a 100 miles away. Shifting gears and merging lanes all happens on the basis of cues that trigger the right behavior. Also, beliefs and morality, adopted over the years, cause people to behave in certain ways. They prescribe what they should or should not do. Making a gift to a charity when receiving a mailing, is an example, as is the general politeness shown other people.

Feelings, moods and ambitions, as well as expectations can trigger behavior and the way people respond to events. You might recognize the behavior of eating a favorite snack when you are in a blue mood. The cue could also be other people, their words or actions, or circumstances and events. Consider the neighbor who always seems to push your buttons, or the feeling of excitement when you receive an invitation to a party. Through the ages demagogues have effectively employed these and other mental principles, and have been able to mold entire groups of people according to their will.

These responses cannot be labeled either good or bad. They just are what they are: responses triggered by a cue. They make your everyday life run smoothly according to more or less predictable paths. Just as an object falls to the ground when you drop it, so will people respond in predictable ways to certain cues.

This does not mean that certain effects are unavoidable. You can always counteract the principle that is at work with another principle. In the physical world this would mean that you catch the object before it hits the floor, or attach a string to it so it will stop in mid air. In the mental world it means you can intercept an automatic response by preparing an alternative way to respond ahead of time. This is called behavior modification and it is well known in the world of psychology. Various kinds of therapies make use of behavior modification techniques.

Principles from both the physical and mental worlds are operative at all times. They work regardless of the time of year or time of day. They operate for all people, irrespective of their age, gender, standing or nationality. More often than not, several principles are at work at the same time. A second principle can either reinforce or counteract the effect of the first one. This makes for a complex process that is not always easy to analyze correctly.

Spiritual principles operate on the same basis: at all times, for all of humanity, and usually combined. Some people call them laws, to indicate their reliability. Since the word "law" has a punitive quality to it, as in "law and order", I prefer to use the word principle. It points to the operative quality, without any connotation of punishment or judgment.

To search for spiritual principles, to find out what they are and whether they are true or not, is a journey in its own right. The answers to spiritual questions will not be as clear cut as the answers might be to similar questions about the physical and mental worlds. In the spiritual world there are no neat mathematical formulas, nor equations that irrefutably prove the validity of a principle. Still, there is one way to discover how spiritual principles operate. That is the way of experience. When you, knowingly or unknowingly, apply a principle you experience its effect. In a way, a repeated "throw, wait, BANG!" teaches how a principle operates in the spiritual world. Just as a toddler learns by doing, so does a parent. Your experience will show you the working of spiritual principles.

Out of pure curiosity, humankind has found, and is still seeking to know, the operative principles of the physical world. Psychologists and therapists of all kind, out of pure therapeutic necessity, have discovered, and are still exploring, the operative principles of the mental world. Each of us, individually, is called to become aware of the operative principles of the spiritual world, the home of the essence of our being. You are called to become aware of the way spiritual principles are working in your life and in your relationships.

Parents in particular can benefit from knowing the workings of the spiritual world. Many times parents face situations and problems that do not seem to have a solution on either the physical or the mental level.

Whether the issue is disobedience, sibling fights, learning disabilities or illness, to name just a few, parents greatly benefit when they gain a new perspective. A perspective that lets them look beyond the appearance of the problem to what lies beyond, namely the spiritual reality that is the basis of life. When you are aware of the spiritual principles that are operative in your life, it is easier to look past the outer appearance. You identify the appearance as just an appearance and recognize the spiritual truth that lies beyond. An example might shed some light on this.

Consider the insistent whining of a child, mentioned before. On the surface it looks as if the child just wants to whine for the sake of whining. If we look at it an instant longer we may find that he is just at the end of his rope and needs a nap. It is also possible that by whining the child is actually asking for clear boundaries of behavior. On many occasions insight into child development and children's mental abilities will direct you in finding a way to deal with whining. But there are times when you need to open yourself to the reality beyond this mental reality. Then you might discover the child's longing for love, his longing to be connected to the parent. In those instances no measure, no solution will bring relief to the child, nor to the parent, but the sincere involvement of the parent in the child's life. Beyond the outer appearance of whining lies the spiritual need to be loved.

Other recurring problems in family life, like children's fights, disagreements, anger and disobedience do not have to remain problems. They can become challenges to respond in ways that recognize the physical, mental and spiritual realities of all people involved. These issues and others are the subjects of Chapters 9 and 10.

You can learn more about the spiritual principles by reading about them in religious and mystical writings. When drawn to a certain principle, you may come upon it in more than one source, put differently. Jesus' emphasis on Love ("Love one another as I have loved you") finds an echo in the 14th Dalai Lama's teaching of kindness and compassion. It is noteworthy that Jesus did not hand his listeners a clear cut formula. He used stories, or parables to introduce spiritual ideas. He preferred to give people the feel for an idea, to show them the underlying intent. The same is true of other teachings. Hinduism abounds with stories. The Bhagavad Gita is not a dry theory, it is a tale full of action and emotion. The real message is found beyond the words. When you read these and other stories, look beyond the occurrences described. You can distill from them spiritual principles that are operative in the lives of people then as well as today.

There are many spiritual principles and sub-principles. In his book "Your Life. Why It Is the Way It Is and What You Can Do About It", Bruce McArthur recognizes 32 different "universal laws". He mentions e.g., *Like begets like*, *There is nothing by chance* and *Ask the Spirit, with faith, and you will receive.* Deepak Chopra describes seven laws of life in his book "The Seven Spiritual Laws of Success", among which are *The law of pure potentiality* and *The law of "Dharma" or purpose in life.* Mystics and writers try to capture in words the essence of spiritual principles in a way that makes sense to them and to the people they address. You can do the same. This chapter will help you make a start by introducing three spiritual principles, namely *Love, Pure intention* and *Expectancy*. I chose these three principles because their working is so clearly visible in the parent-child relationship.

LOVE

The first spiritual principle is the principle of *Love*. It is the cornerstone of spiritual life. All mystic and religious writings emphasize love in its various expressions. In "Ocean of Wisdom" the 14th Dalai Lama of Tibet says: "My mission is the practice of compassion, love, and kindness." The Bhagavad Gita, a centuries old Sanskrit mystical text, says: "By love he knows me in truth, who I am and what I am." In the introduction to his English translation of the Bhagavad Gita, scholar Juan Mascaro writes: "Many are the themes of the symphony of the Bhagavad Gita, but the central ones are three: Light, love and life."

The Bible's New Testament contains a letter from the apostle Paul to his friends in the city of Corinth. He writes about Love:

> *"Love is patient; love is kind and envies no one. Love is never boastful, nor conceited, nor rude; never selfish, not quick to take offense. Love keeps no score of wrongs; does not gloat over other men's sins, but delights in the truth. There is nothing love cannot face; there is no limit to its faith, its hope, and its endurance. Love will never come to an end. ... In a word, there are three things that last for ever: faith, hope, and love; but the greatest of them all is love."*

(1Cor.13)

These words express the essence of spiritual life. And the key word is Love.

Bruce McArthur, in his book mentioned earlier, also talks about Love. The book is based on extensive research of American psychic Edgar Cayce's work. From the readings Bruce McArthur gleaned the spiritual principles that Edgar Cayce felt are operative in life. The result is a valuable handbook, introducing various principles one at a time and guiding the reader through a personal transformation. About Love he writes:

> *"Love transforms. It is perhaps the simplest of all the laws. It means that no matter what kind of a condition, situation, or relationship you are dealing with, when you bring love to that circumstance of life, it will change, it will be lifted, it will be transformed. ... Love transforms because it is the presence of God! It's not that God loves, but that GOD IS LOVE. **The experience of love is the way in which you sense and touch the Presence within.** As you accept the Presence within - the love within you - and focus it on aspects of your life, it transforms because it is pure creative force. It is the power of life available to you. It will transform anywhere, anytime, any condition, and any situation to which you apply it."*
> *(Author's emphasis)*
>
> "Your Life. Why It Is the Way It Is and What
> You Can Do About It", by Bruce McArthur

Think and reflect on what McArthur says here: *to experience love is to experience God!* Or: *You experience God when you love!* Parents are lucky. As a parent you have a unique opportunity before you. By loving your very own little ones you put into practice the principle of Love. What is more natural for a parent than to hold, hug, cuddle, fondle and play with a baby? It is a timeless image and it bespeaks the wisdom of Life to give you an opportunity, right in your own lap, to put yourself under the principle of Love. Because, *as you accept the love within you and focus it on aspects of your life, it transforms. Love transforms anywhere, anytime, anything.*

To be loved, to feel the love of others is heart warming, encouraging, and healing. Being loved is like being lighted on the way. But *to love* is to discover that *you* are the one who is holding the light. Through loving you transform to become the light.

By loving your babies and children so naturally and almost in spite of yourself, you have the opportunity to place yourself under the governance of the principle of Love. And through that activity you transform yourself. There is no room for fear when you love. There is no room for resentment when you love, no room for despair and desolation. The chance to love a child is the chance to let love become part of your life, and let that love shine through in everything you do.

PURE INTENTION

Closely connected to the principle of transforming love is the principle of *pure intention.* It relates to the *Why?* of our actions. When exploring spiritual works you will come across this principle many times. In a documentary about her life and work, when talking about donations, Mother Theresa says: "It does not matter how much you give. What matters is the amount of love with which you give it." That means a departure from the regular approach of checks and balances. What matters more than the actual dollar amount given, is *your intention* behind it, namely to love the people and the cause to which you give. Thought provoking as her words may be, they are not really new.

Listen to Luke's report of Jesus' teaching in the story of the poor widow:

> *"He [Jesus] looked up and saw the rich people dropping their gifts into the chest of the temple treasury; and he noticed a poor widow putting in two tiny coins. "I tell you this," he said: "this poor widow has given more than any of them; for those others who have given had more than enough, but she, with less than enough, has given all she had to live on."*

(Lk 21:1-4)

This story clearly emphasizes Jesus' preference for quality over quantity, for intention over effect.

Not just the teaching in the Bible recognizes the spiritual principle of pure intention. So does Buddhism. In an effort to contribute to worldwide interreligious dialogue, scholar on comparative religions Richard H. Drummond writes:

> *"... the Buddha's teaching is concerned to insist that the ethical quality of human intent and motives, thoughts, and attitudes is as important personally and cosmically as external words and deeds. Indeed, the range of the teaching makes clear that the Buddha perceived the inner dimension to be primarily significant and determinative."*

"A Broader Vision. Perspectives on the Buddha and the Christ", by
Richard H. Drummond

It is not surprising then to see the principle of pure intention also present in the teaching of the 14th Dalai Lama of Tibet. He says:

> *"I feel that the essence of all spiritual life is your emotion, your attitude toward others. Once you have pure and sincere motivation, all the rest follows. You can develop this right attitude toward others on the basis of kindness, love, and respect, and on the clear realization of the oneness of all human beings. This is important because others benefit by this motivation as much as anything we do. Then, with a pure heart, you can carry on any work - farming, mechanical engineering, working as a doctor, as a lawyer, as a teacher - and your profession becomes a real instrument to help the human community."*

"Ocean of Wisdom", by the 14th Dalai Lama of Tibet

Thinking along this line you can "carry on" with parenting with a pure heart and it will become a real instrument to help your family members. To become clear about your motivation, and thus make your heart pure, work with your spiritual ideal and the attitudes and actions that flow from it. Your framework of ideals is the tool that enables you to put into practice the principle of pure intention. The reason why a pure intention is so important, is that it is stable, enduring and reliable. Physical effects, purchases, achievements, standing, etc., can only go so far in satisfying a person's hunger. But a pure intention leads to true food for the soul that lasts forever. When outer appearances have had their time and are no longer here, your pure intention is still with you. It will shine through in the activities you engage in next, and it lies at the basis of your future accomplishments.

When the apostle Paul writes about Love, in the same letter quoted earlier, he also alludes to the *intention* to love:

> *"I may speak in tongues of men or of angels, but if I am*
> *without love, I am a sounding gong or a clanging*
> *cymbal. I may have the gift of prophecy, and know every*
> *hidden truth; I may have faith strong enough to move*
> *mountains; but if I have no love, I am nothing. I may dole*
> *out all I possess, or even give my body to be burnt, but if I*
> *have no love, I am none the better."*
>
> (1Cor.13:1-3)

If your intention is anything other than to love, it is of no use. Especially in the relationship with your children, it can be helpful to keep this in mind: You may be right, you may have common sense on your side, but if you forget your *intention to* first of all *love* your child, *it means nothing.* What then, does it mean to love your child in the middle of a disagreement? It means to heed Paul's advice, by deciding "not to take offense", and "not to keep a score of wrongs." It means to commit yourself to finding out who you are and what it means to be a parent. It means to translate that awareness into a new attitude towards your children. It means to be willing to change and grow.

EXPECTANCY

The principle of intention, in its turn, is closely connected to the principle of *faith,* of *expectancy.* The expression "a self fulfilling prophecy" alludes to this principle. Also, some have turned the well known saying "seeing is believing" around as to become "you will see it when you believe it." Both point to your frame of mind. If you fear disaster, disaster will befall you. But if you expect to have a good experience, you will focus on those conditions that bring about a good experience. Expectancy carries with it the quality of openness. Fearing disaster is like looking into a funnel downwards. You close yourself off by looking in only one direction. On the other hand, to expect good to happen is like looking through a funnel upwards. The light can shine on you from various angles.

Jesus used the analogy of a child to explain the principle of expectancy:

> *"They even brought babies for him to touch. When the disciples saw them they rebuked them, but Jesus called for the children and said, 'Let the little ones come to me; do not try to stop them; for the kingdom of God belongs to such as these. I tell you that whoever does not accept the kingdom of God like a child will never enter it.'"*

(Lk 18:15-17)

Jesus calls on us to emulate the attitude of a small child that does not worry about where it is going. A child does not worry whether she will be cared for tomorrow as long as she firmly holds the parent's hand. The attitude of an expectant child speaks of hope, and trust, of susceptibility to accept new ways.

In dealing with their children parents expect them to be susceptible to their guidelines. As a parent you expect and demand that your children trust you. You were a child once yourself, and these things were expected of you too. However, as you grew older you learned to take on more responsibility for your decisions. It seems contradictory to adopt a childlike attitude at this time. The point is, that right in the middle of your decision making and right in the middle of carrying out your responsibilities, you look for direction from within. You are called to adopt this attitude towards life: to know that Love is the essence of Life and to expect and trust Life to guide you on our path.

Love, Pure intention and Expectancy. There are many more spiritual principles, as you will no doubt discover. At first they may sound vague and remote, just as the principles discussed here did on the outset. However nebulous they may appear to be at first glance, once you read about them, you will get a feel for what they mean. And when you test and apply them, your knowledge of these principles will shed much needed light on daily occurring situations that trouble you. (In the bibliography you can find titles of several books that define and explore spiritual principles.)

Gaining knowledge about the spiritual world and its principles is a first step. It shows your willingness to recognize that there is more to the world than solely its appearance. But you will need to take it one step further. It is necessary to reflect upon the gathered information and ponder it. The answers that satisfy your curiosity have to ring true in your deepest self, in your inner being. Reflection, pondering and contemplation. These form the next step on the road called *turning within*.

TURNING WITHIN

Turning within is expecting answers and clues to come from your inner being. You look for direction within yourself, as opposed to expecting other people or outside developments to direct you and to motivate and challenge you. Within is found the fount of life. Life, Spirit, God, expresses itself as you and me, and through you and me.

To help you understand this statement, consider a tree and its branches. The tree's sap, the life force of the tree, runs through the very center of the branches, and nourishes them, independent of weather conditions. You are like a branch. In the very center of you there is the contact point with the Life Force, and that Life Force sustains you and nourishes you. It directs the way you grow. Branches on a tree produce leaves, blossom, fruit and seed, all by the grace of their connection with the tree. Turning within means to acknowledge that just as the Life Force runs through the tree, it runs through you, too. When you turn within you can expect to see and feel the life sap flow, you can expect to blossom and bear fruit too.

What exactly is this "life sap"? In essence it is the one Force, the one Energy that permeates the whole of Creation. Just as the Lord our God is one, so is His Energy. There is only one God and there is only one Energy. All the energy and force we experience and witness all around us, are the one Energy of the one God. Creation is the one Energy expressed in individual being, action, experience. The energy that forms a new body in a mother's womb is God's Energy. The energy that makes hearts pump, blood flow and brains function, is God's Energy. The basic energy with which people live their daily lives, and with which they accomplish little and big things, is all this very same divine Energy. When working or playing, whenever people extend energy, they let the Force flow. Unconsciously they draw upon the life sap.

Even when you experience a force that you interpret as negative, you can still be sure of its true origin: God Force, God Energy. It may be misdirected or handled badly, but it remains God's Energy. It does not come from some remote source or from some alien people. The one source of all power and energy is God. There is no need to be afraid. Per definition, there can never be more than that one Energy, that one Power at work.

Mystic writings, and very specifically the Edgar Cayce works, explain that each individual being has direct access to God and to this God-sent Power through the inner chamber. Within each and every one of us lies the connection to the One Force of the One God, or the Creative Force. (The plural form, Creative Forces, is used as well. The plural form indicates diversity of expression, not diversity of origin).

It is important to know that every individual has access to the Creative Forces, without having to go through an intermediary, like a teacher, minister, guru, etc. Each of us can learn to draw consciously and methodically upon that Force. On a daily basis, on an hourly basis, and whenever the need arises, each of us can draw upon the Energy that is of God. Direct communication with God is possible, always and everywhere. Turning within is the way in which to consciously invite God's Energy into your life.

In his book quoted earlier, Bruce McArthur uses a splendid allegory to illustrate the power that is stored within:

> *"Let's use a modern hydroelectric installation as an analogy. The water held in the reservoir behind a huge dam is stored energy; love is also a tremendous store of energy available to us and within us. The stored water makes the reservoir a beautiful place to be and to enjoy. However, the reservoir's full potential isn't realized until the water is released through the dam's gates, flows through turbines which drive the generators to*

*produce electricity, which in turn flows through
transmission lines. Then power, heat, and light for homes
and industry are provided. The water discharged from the
turbines also forms a river which provides recreation,
fishing and irrigation for crops. It is transforming
because it gives life to the land and those dependent on it.
....The key to the process of opening the gates is for you to
recognize and to love that source of love within. As you
do, you are able to open yourself and to increase the flow
through you to the world.
This is a key. If you don't give attention to the source of
love within you - the Spirit within - it is as if it didn't exist,
because it makes no demands on you. Yet it is the
greatest power of the Universe, in infinite supply within
you, waiting for you to release it and let it flow. When
you make the choice to open the gate and release that
supply, you begin by accepting the love which is the God
Presence within."*

"Your Life. Why It Is the Way It Is and What
You Can Do About It", by Bruce McArthur

Turning within is the way to open the inner door to let
the Creative Forces flow. When you become cut off from
the flow, like a dried out riverbed, you wither and die
spiritually.

Parents cannot afford to be cut off from the flow of life,
from the flow of inspiration. Parents need a place of rest
to come back to, to find peace and feel renewed
dedication. Then, when stepping back into the world
with its daily occurrences and problems, they will receive
guidance to do what works best for all involved. That
way, both parents and children benefit. The joys as
well as the pressures of parenthood are calls to turn
within.

Within is found the fount of life, from which you ladle out blessings to both your children and yourself.

You have recently defined your spiritual ideal and have found a way to apply what you hold dearly in your daily life and especially in the contact with your children. Now it is even more important to have continuous access to the Creative Forces. By your commitment to let your decisions be guided by the chosen spiritual ideal, you have consciously chosen to let yourself be guided by what is true in spiritual terms. The mental and physical realities are still there, of course, but as motivators they have taken a back seat. From now on the spiritual reality takes precedence. For most of us, this is a new way of living. It is easy to let old habits and attitudes take back their former places. To be reminded and inspired to continue on the chosen track it is paramount to be in contact with spiritual reality on a continual basis. Turning within lets you do just that.

The way to turn within is to deliberately tune out to the signals of the world around you and concentrate on your inner being through prayer and meditation. These are instruments of preparation. Their inward and contemplative character forms the necessary counterpart to the active and sometimes groundbreaking application of ideals.

APPLICATION

1. Do you have a preferred name for the unnamable, the creative force, that we all feel is central to our lives? Play around with a few alternative wordings and write down the ones that appeal to you.

2. For the sake of clarification this book talks about the physical world, the mental world and the spiritual world, each with its own operative principles. These three worlds together make up the world in which you live. Does it appear likely to you that there are spiritual principles operative in your life that are just as consequential as are more readily identifiable principles?
   Try to think of spiritual principles other than the ones mentioned in this chapter.

3. The last section talks about each person having direct access to Spirit (Life, God) without having to go through an intermediary. Have you ever experienced direct contact with the Divine in any of the forms in which it may have expressed? (e.g., The flash of an insight or vision, feeling connected to nature, in prayer, in the love shared between people, etc.)

4. To many people the prospect of having to sit alone in quiet contemplation is not very appealing. Do you recognize this?

   Now that you have read about it, are you willing to give turning within a try?

5

PRAYER

When you get to the place where you would
worry ... stop and pray!
For why worry, when you can pray?

Edgar Cayce

PRAYER AND RELEASE

Prayer is a monologue in which you address Spirit (God, the Creative Forces). Whether alone or in a group, you try to express in words what goes on in and around you. You may say the words aloud, or think them. Prayer is a means to address Spirit and find words for inner thoughts, worries, fears, impressions, considerations, gratefulness, hopes, desires, etc.

You might wonder what prayer does, and why it would make sense to spend time to talk about yourself and others. It is interesting to read what Jesus says about prayer. According to him "Your Father knows the things you need before you ask them" (Mt. 6:8). In this light any kind of prayer seems superfluous, some kind of performance you put on for yourself and for the ones who might be with you. On the other hand, Jesus assures us that if we ask and keep on asking we will receive. There is a contradiction here. First he implies that it is pointless to ask, because God already knows our needs. And then he tells us to persevere in asking. How can we reconcile this contradiction?

The answer lies in what happens when you pray. The answer lies in the process that takes place within you when you talk about your life in prayer. When you pray and talk about your concerns and worries, you bring them all before God, before Life. You pour out feelings of guilt, of insecurity, of powerlessness. You talk about your anger and frustration. You release and place all anxiety in Life's hands, on God's altar. Prayer makes a clean sweep. It empties you. By praying and keeping on praying you empty yourself of concern and anxiety. And that is the first thing that needs to happen when embarking on a journey into the inner world. The brush called prayer clears out the inner room. Prayer sweeps debris, remnants and other unneeded material into a pile, and disposes of it properly.

This does not mean that all problems vanish right away, nor does it mean that by handing over the responsibility for them you are no longer committed to resolving them. It simply means that by emptying yourself you make room for Spirit (God, Life) to enter into your experience. If you keep yourself filled with concern and worry, there will be no room left for God to work through you, for Life to flow. But why would you want to burden Spirit with your troubles? Why would Spirit be interested? What can

Life do about them? To answer these legitimate questions let's first examine our relationship with Spirit (God, Life).

Spirit expresses Itself in individual being, in you and in me. All individuals, as well as the whole array of other creations, are Spirit individually expressed. Spirit is the lifeblood of all, always and everywhere. We are Spirit made manifest. We cannot be separated from Spirit. But what we *can* do, is *think* that we are separate from Spirit by imagining that we are not connected. We reinforce the sense of separation by insisting to look in the opposite direction, namely by adopting a selfish attitude and by holding on to feelings of fear and guilt, etc. But there never really has been any separation. The view from our perspective has just become cloudy. Not only do we not see or feel Life at its fullest, we see problems and troubles all around us. These are real to us. Yet Spirit knows how to dissolve these appearances with a mere ray of Light. That can happen in our experience too, if only we let it be so. By the act of praying, we acknowledge our connection to the Source of Life. We acknowledge that the images of troubles and problems are due to a limited perspective. We do not burden God with our worries; he sweeps them off the table. But that can only happen if we put them there.

Offering your worries and anxieties to Life, laying them on the altar of God, takes them out of your heart. They are no longer your responsibility; they actually never have been. The only responsibility you have ever had, have now, and will ever have is to be a channel through which God's Love can flow into the world.

GUIDELINES FOR PRAYER

Jesus' disciples at one point became painfully aware of how poorly their own way of prayer compared to their master's. Then they asked him how to pray. He answered them by saying a short prayer, which we have come to call The Lord's Prayer:

> *"Our Father in heaven,*
> *thy name be hallowed;*
> *thy kingdom come,*
> *thy will be done,*
> *on earth as in heaven.*
> *Give us today our daily bread.*
> *Forgive us the wrong we have done,*
> *as we have forgiven those who have wronged us.*
> *And do not bring us to the test,*
> *but save us from the evil one.*
> *For thine is the kingdom*
> *and the power and the glory, for ever.*
> *Amen."*

(Mt. 6:9-13, Lk. 11:2-4)

It is interesting that Jesus does not explain to them how to pray. He simply gives an example, and a rather short one at that. On another occasion he rebukes the hypocrites who pray on the corner of the street so all may see how pious they are. Then he explains that true prayer takes place in the inner chamber, behind closed doors, where no one else can come (Mt.6:5). He himself would often go and pray alone at the quietest time possible, long before sunrise. Clearly Jesus spent a lot of time in prayer. When it is almost time for him to go, he prays for the completion of his mission through his followers. And he worries for their sake. In prayer he voices all his concern and puts it on the altar.

> *"I finished the work you gave me to do. I brought you glory on earth. You gave me some men from the world. I gave these men the teachings that you gave me, and they accepted those teachings. I pray for them now. Now I am coming to you. I will not stay in the world now. But these men are still in the world. Holy Father, keep them safe by the power of your name. Make them ready for your service through your truth."*

(excerpts from John 17)

Then, just before the soldiers come to take him away, he takes three followers with him and instructs them to be watchful. Then he continues on alone, and prays. He voices his anguish and asks that the cup of suffering may pass. But he quickly follows that request with: "yet, not my will but Thine be done" (Mk. 14:34-36, Lk. 22:42). After releasing his fear and anxiety Jesus makes room in himself to become a channel for Spirit to work through him. By declaring "Your will be done" he leaves behind his personal interpretation of the situation. He distances himself from the ego-perspective and aligns himself with the flow of Life, to go the way of the Spirit.

These examples reveal some important features of prayer that we can look at now:

— *Prayer is private business.* Even when praying in a group, prayer remains an individual matter. You cannot borrow the intent of another, or ride the wave of another person's experience.

- *Prayer is an ongoing activity.* It is necessary to acknowledge again and again that we are connected to God.

- *Prayer is release.* You pour out all concern in prayer, release it and place it in God's hands. You empty yourself of all obstacles to receiving the Light.

- *Prayer is declaring allegiance to the way of the Spirit.* When you say "Your will be done" you make known your intent to receive guidance and follow it.

The point of prayer lies in its function as a total exterminator of worries. When Jesus says: "Unless you become as children you cannot enter the Kingdom of God," he means: Unless you become free of worry, free of concern, trusting Abba, you cannot come in the flow of Life, you cannot follow the way of the Spirit. Prayer is the means by which you attain that freedom, by placing all before Him. When that is accomplished you are relieved, you feel a lightness coming over you. Now you are ready to enter into the "Kingdom of God", just as Jesus promises. When the heavy blanket of concern and fear no longer burdens you, the Light can shine on you and through you. Praying is a necessary preparation for receiving the Light.

APPLICATION

You will now concentrate on writing your own prayer. You yourself will choose what to put in it. There is nothing magical about the words used in prayer. The Lord's Prayer or any other prayer can easily become a routine without any inner experience. The words themselves are hollow.

You are the one who infuses them with meaning. The words you choose can be few or many, specific or general. You can borrow lines from an existing prayer or compose your own. It does not matter. What matters is that the words allow you to connect to the value beyond of which they remind you.

1. Opening. Start your prayer by addressing God (Spirit, or the name you prefer).
   I personally like to use the well-known *Our Father, who art in heaven.* With this opening there is no doubt to whom I am talking. The addressee, *Our Father*, is not just my prerogative. *Our* means that all of Creation has access to him. *Father* stands for the origin and destination of all. The address *Heaven* to me means perfection, unity, bliss. This little sentence, so easily said by rote, can prove to be the key to open the door to a world of meaning. Spirit is where we all come from and where we all are going. Perfection and Oneness are our origin and our destination.

   Think about an opening that appeals to you. You might like to start your prayer with *Father-Mother-God, Life* or *All present Spirit.* Play around with possible beginnings. Write down the ones you like.

2. Next, acknowledge that life is an opportunity, a gift. The world is an opportunity and a gift. You and I are a gift, as well as all the people around us (though it may not always feel that way!). So, you could say something like: *Thank you for all that you have given me.* (*all* meaning the good and the bad, the beautiful and the ugly.)

   You could gratefully mention the members of your family, each individually, as well as some of your relatives and friends or colleagues that you have come into contact with that day or that week. Try to find words that express your being grateful for life and its people and experiences.

3. Next are problem situations, difficult encounters or otherwise troubling issues. Put them all in a basket and place it on the table to be taken away (release). Ask that on the right moment you may know what to say or do, or *not* to say and *not* to do. Examples of ways to express this thought:

   - *I present you now with* ...(issue)... *which is troubling me a lot,* or

   - *I am thinking about* ...(problem)... *and* ...(people involved)... *and place them all in your hands*

   and continue with, for instance:

   - *They are part of Life, and thus part of you. They are in your hands, not mine. Please show me what is the right attitude,* or

— *I do not want to be tied up in it personally. You, Life, know what is best for all involved. Please show me the way*

See if you can find ways to capture these thoughts in your own words.

4. If you really think about it, does it make sense to follow your worldly personality, your own ego in its little schemes and detours? They only leave you groping in the dark. Instead you could be in the full light heading towards perfection, unity and bliss. So at the end of your prayer you could state your commitment to follow Spirit guidance by saying, for example:

— *Your will be done in me and through me,* or

— *Let me be a channel of help and blessing*

Write down your own commitment.

5. Now put it all together. With each section read the answer you put down and reflect on it. Then decide how you want to phrase the thought and put it down on a clean sheet of paper. You could also use the format on page 102.

Here, as with the target of ideals, the words you choose are not set in stone. Putting down your thoughts in writing helps you to become aware of your inner intent. It will become clearer to you which path you want to take. At a later time you might very well feel that you need to adjust this prayer to better reflect your intent.

YOUR OWN PRAYER

Opening
(e.g., *Our Father
in Heaven,
Father-Mother-
God*, etc.)

Give thanks
for life and
people around
you

Empty yourself
of worries

Close with
commitment to
follow the way
of the Spirit

6

MEDITATION

As you may experience in some of your moments of meditation, finding peace within enables you to give more assurance, more help to others...
...as harmony and beauty and grace reign within your consciousness, you give that to others - and others wonder what moved them to feel differently ... This is the manner in which the spirit of truth operates.

Edgar Cayce

YOUR INNER ROOM

In the previous chapter you read about the function of prayer as a brush that cleans the inner room. When you pray you purge yourself of all anxiety and concern. You lift the heavy blanket of worry and despair. You empty and cleanse the inner room. This is a necessary preparation for receiving the Light. To receive the Light you linger in that cleansed inner space for a while and invite the Creative Forces in. This is called meditation. Meditation is the key that opens the door to let the

Creative Forces in. As soon as you turn the key and open the inner door the Creative Forces will seize the opportunity and start to flow through you. You might feel this at the time, or you might not. It does not matter, either way. The fact is, you have opened the door for the Creative Forces to flow through you and that is what is going to happen. By emptying yourself through prayer you make room for God to come in. With the key called meditation you are able to connect and stay connected to God, so you can let yourself be filled with God's Energy. Over time you will be able to notice a deepening of the quality of your life. Then you will recognize what brought that about: the cleansed inner space.

Let's look at an analogy. Consider changing the oil in your car. You take the car to the shop or you park it in a flat spot. You open the valve to let the used oil run out and catch it in a container. This is all very similar to what happens when you pray. Gathered with others or alone, you empty yourself and place all concern in God's hands. Now, back to the oil and the car. You close the valve and pour in fresh new oil. Imagine what would happen if you forgot to do that! The same holds for us. This is the perfect time to fill up with fresh new energy. When prayer has helped to empty out and clean up, the word of God can enter in. Where prayer is pouring out, meditation is pouring in. Where prayer is talking, meditation is listening.

GUIDELINES FOR MEDITATION

Various methods of meditation exist. There is not one right way to enter into this contemplative state. You are capable of choosing the form that is most suitable for you. To explore various styles it can be helpful to read about meditation. In the bibliography you will find a list of books about meditation and related matters that can be helpful in this respect.   What follows now is a basic outline of the practice of meditation.

At the outset it is important to state that two attitudes are essential to the practice of meditation:

− A strong and sincere desire to seek truth, to be connected to God
− A commitment to a constant, consistent effort

You are already familiar with the first attitude, the sincere desire to connect with the Source. It is your passport and constant companion on the road to fulfillment. You will only become aware of the need for the second attitude, a constant and consistent effort, when you experience what your life is like when you   practice meditation on a daily basis for a period of time. It is a catch-22, and the best thing to do is to give it a try.

There are no exclusives in meditation, and there is no one right way to meditate. Experiment and discover for yourself what your own best way to meditate is. Therefore, look upon this outline as a suggestion, and feel free to experiment:

−   Pick a time of day that you think you are least likely to be disturbed or distracted. Some recommend a time in the middle of the night, others prefer to meditate upon rising. Clearly parents of young children do not really have any time when they will not be disturbed or distracted, or not fall asleep!   Experiment with a few time slots: just before bedtime, children's nap time, upon rising, etc. Then pick one, and stick with it. From now on, every day, this particular time is set aside. This is your quiet time.

– Bathe, or take a shower. Edgar Cayce said the following about the preparation for meditation:

> *"... before true meditation we must be clean in body and mind so that we may be fit to meet the Lord"*
>
> "A Search for God", by Edgar Cayce

The book goes on to say that our physical, mental and spiritual bodies "are so closely knit together that the impressions of one have their effects upon the other two." You will have to discover on your own what it takes to prepare yourself in body and mind. I always feel rejuvenated after taking a shower. Not only is my skin cleansed, but it feels as if the spray has washed away the troubles of the day.

– Choose a place to meditate. If you use one particular place consistently, your mind will associate it with contemplation, and it becomes easier to focus your mind. Make sure you are not wearing anything tight. Wear loose, comfortable clothing. Lie down, or sit in a comfortable position: straight back, hands in your lap. Close your eyes.

– Empty the conscious mind through prayer. Purge yourself of all hindrances that would block the communication with the Source. The Creative Force is spiritual force and it can only be sought by our spiritual body. Release the issues of the physical body and the mind. Each of us will develop a sense of what is necessary to "straighten the way for the Lord."

– Choose a meditation statement, or affirmation. (Later in this chapter, in the sections on affirmations, you will learn how to arrive at a meaningful statement to use in meditation.)

Think or say the statement a few times, concentrating on the value beyond the words. Then pause, and stay quiet and attentive. Meditation is an activity of feeling, of sensing the spirit of truth. Concentrating on an inspiring thought will help you reach the highest possible state of awareness of which you are capable. Simply reciting and repeating statements will not take you there.

Thoughts will pop into your mind that have nothing to do with your meditation. Do not worry about it, just call your attention back to the truth you were contemplating. Think or say the statement again. Every time your mind wanders off on some tangent, gently bring it back. Gradually your mind will get used to the practice of meditation, and it will become less difficult to stay in an attentive, receptive state.

– Some writings recommend a breathing pattern, similar to the one practiced in yoga. Experiment, and see for yourself what feels right.

– The time spent in meditation varies. When you are still getting used to meditating I suggest you spend five to ten minutes each day at your set quiet time. Later on you could expand it to your liking by increasing the duration or by setting aside two or more quiet times in a day. Joel Goldsmith, an American mystic and author of many books on spiritual life, writes about a "click" he feels when he has connected. According to him the click can come after meditating for some time, or right away. Again, there are no set rules. The essence of meditation lies in what occurs inside of you, not in the faithful following of guidelines. Trust your inner being to direct your efforts.

Not only do meditation methods vary, so do the experiences that people have. Some meditators have reported to feel vibration sensations, coolness of the head, pulsation in the spine, sensation to the eyes, etc., while others do not notice anything in particular. The sensations can be explained by definite physical reactions taking place in our bodies when we meditate, whether we feel it or not. Some suggest that there are contact points between the Spirit Force and the physical body. When we meditate definite physical reactions take place in our bodies through these contact points, the endocrine glands, or chakras. As mentioned earlier, some people actually feel these changes taking place while meditating. A discussion of what actually occurs in the chakras lies beyond the scope of this work. (If this aspect of meditation interests you, consult the bibliography at the end of this book.)

The point is not to get distracted by these sensations. They are signposts, telling you that you are on the way. They are not the goal you seek. You acknowledge the occurrence and then move forward toward the Source.

You were made in the image of our Maker. Your spiritual body has never left spiritual reality, it is ever in the presence of God. To become aware of this and to let the Creative Force permeate your being, use prayer and meditation to consciously turn your mind and body in the direction of the Light.

A PRAYERFUL ATTITUDE

To clarify any misunderstanding it is important to say that whatever definitions of prayer and meditation are in use, the exact name of the practice is not what matters. What really matters is the sincere intent to attune oneself to God, to connect with the inner being. You might want to call confession prayer, or include praise and expressing gratitude. Another argues that contemplation and meditation are both a form of prayer. Or walking in nature, or listening to music. It does not matter. What counts is the purpose of communicating with the Spirit within. Every person has a unique, individual way of achieving that. We use distinctions only for clarifying the process by which we might establish this communication.

Maybe it would be best to bunch all definitions together and call it a prayerful attitude. A prayerful attitude can be achieved even in the middle of a group of rambunctious kindergartners, or during a walk around the block, as well as at the set quiet time. A prayerful attitude is an attitude characterized by openness, receptivity and willingness, and by the recognition of the all encompassing presence of the Spirit. And with this attitude you can sing praise, be grateful, confess, think of others, contemplate, reflect and meditate. The whole array of spiritual expression is possible when you adopt a prayerful attitude.

This reminds me of an experience from my childhood. One memory is pictured very clearly in my mind. I must have been eight or nine at the time. My sister Lizet and I are staying at my grandparents' house for a week's vacation. Grandfather, Grandmother, Lizet and I are sitting at the breakfast table. We have just finished eating, and the sun's rays fall through the window-panes on the white table cloth. There my grandfather's pale hands lie, folded in prayer. With eyes closed he pronounces the names of each of his four children and their spouses and his (then) sixteen grandchildren, pausing with each name. Once in a while he adds a thought to release any anxiety he feels about an issue facing the person he just mentioned. My sister and I both listen quietly, awed by his radiant presence. He thus prayed every morning.

AFFIRMATIONS

In the guidelines for meditation the word "affirmation" was mentioned. What exactly is an affirmation?

An affirmation is a "firm-maker." It turns a jelly matter into a solid substance. It anchors an idea that might otherwise drift away. An affirmation is a sentence in which you put into words the essence of a thought. It puts into tangible form a thought that quickens your mind and soul. It does so because it speaks directly to your inner being, your spiritual body, bypassing all ego-wishes and distracting thoughts. It speaks directly to your inner being and it reaffirms an insight that is on the edge of your conscious mind. It inspires and challenges. The insight is right at the outer edge of your understanding. Because of that it is easy to forget what it exactly looked and felt like, if it is not pulled back on center stage, again and again. Also, leading a busy life is not conducive to entertaining lofty thoughts. It takes a conscious effort to remember. An affirmation helps to recapture again and again the insight you are working with at a particular time. It helps make firm your commitment to Life. An affirmation is like a little hand-drawn map you stick on the dashboard when visiting a place you have never been before. Affirmations are like small "instructions for use" that you keep handy when using a new appliance. Affirmations are handy little gadgets, and your spiritual toolbox becomes more versatile if you have a few at your disposal.

An affirmation is a very personal matter. It expresses an insight that is applicable to you individually. You can work with a few affirmations over a period of time, pertaining to different issues. Certain affirmations might fall away when fully assimilated, while new ones need to be added. Some affirmations may speak to you so directly and clearly that you want to keep them forever.

USING AN AFFIRMATION IN MEDITATION

You can use affirmations in various ways. As mentioned before, one way is to say an affirmation, aloud or in silence, at the start of meditation. This will help focus the mind on the task at hand, namely turning within. Since the affirmation is a spiritual thought that touches the edge of your understanding, it stretches you, it lifts you up. When you deeply feel the essence of the thought captured by the affirmation, your consciousness is raised. Of course, it is not citing the words that does the job, it is the awareness of the thought behind the words that matters. When thinking or saying, and then truly feeling the affirmation, you express your intent to be One with the Source.

When using an affirmation in meditation it is sometimes helpful to repeat it and let the consciousness behind the words wash over you again. Sometimes after thinking or saying an affirmation a thought on the same or related subjects will enter your mind. Savor it and write it down: It is a gift from the Spirit, also called an inspiration!

As far as the choice of an affirmation is concerned, the best thing you can do is to experiment. The place to start is the formulation of your spiritual ideal, since that represents to you the highest understanding of truth and purpose in your life. As explained earlier, your spiritual ideal is a thought that to you represents the highest understanding of truth and purpose in your life. Contemplating this spiritual statement at the start of your meditation, and feeling the essence, the value of it, will help you attune to the Creative Forces. You might want to phrase it differently, so it will flow better for use in meditation. You will come back to this statement again and again, so it is important that it sounds pleasing. Somehow, a flowing, prosaic phrase stimulates the imaginative forces, and those are the very forces that can help focus on the ideal and on attuning to God. A few examples of meditation statements, or affirmations, derived from spiritual ideals, follow. The ideals were taken from the sample list of Chapter 2.

Spiritual ideal	**Affirmation**
To be an agent of peace and truth	*Father-Mother-God, you are peace, you are truth. Let peace and truth shine through me*
To be an innovator	*For you all things are possible; please show me the way*
To be a healer of minds	*Let me be the door through which your peace may flow*
To be a healer of bodies	*We are all made in God's image; we are perfect children of God*
To be a communicator and clarifier of ideas	*God is the sun; we are His radiance. Through him we are connected*
To be a receptive listener	*When others unburden their hearts, let me hold the bowl that receives the outpouring to place it in your hands*
To be a worker for justice and peace	*Lord, show me your ways that lead to justice and peace*

You could also use other statements of truth that strike or inspire you, like:

God's teaching is near you; it is in your mouth and in your heart

(Rom.10:8)

I am sure that nothing can separate us from the love God has for us

(Rom.8:38)

If anyone hears my voice, and opens the door, I will come in and sit down to supper with him and he with me

(Rev.3:20)

There are three things that last forever: faith, hope and love, but the greatest of them all is love

(1Cor.13:13)

A new commandment I give unto you, that you love one another

(John 13:34)

The Lord is good to all men, and his tender care rests upon all his creatures

(Ps.145:9)

Not my will but your will be done in and through me

Edgar Cayce, "A Search for God"

Let me be a channel of blessings, today, now, to those that I contact in every way

Edgar Cayce, "A Search for God"

As the wave is one with the ocean, so I am one with God. As the sunbeam is one with the sun, so I am one with God

Joel Goldsmith, "Conscious Union with God"

All I want is the kingdom of God on earth

Joel Goldsmith, "Conscious Union with God"

God-Life and my life are one. I live, and move, and have my being in God

Joel Goldsmith, "Conscious Union with God"

He's got the whole world in His hands

(Negro spiritual)

May the earth renew itself, and all of our planet's creatures live in peace and harmony

(Greenpeace)

AFFIRMATIONS ON THE SPOT

There is another way to use an affirmation, namely right at the moment when you need a new perspective. Whenever you feel inadequate, threatened, frightened or at a loss, a small affirmation can help you remember Who you really are, and that there is no need to feel powerless. The way I use affirmations is as follows. When I notice that I feel uncomfortable in a situation (ranging from apprehensive to desperate, from slightly blue to depressed) I try to recall some appropriate words, that remind me of what I really am about. For only an instant I take a mental break from the situation. I mentally step outside the situation for a moment and try to let myself be permeated by the meaning of the affirmation. The following examples show you how it works.

When in circumstances that look desperate financially, socially or otherwise, it is very comforting to think:

> *I am not my circumstances*

> I may have created these circumstances, or I may be an accomplice in bringing them about, it does not matter right now. What matters now, is that I am not them. These particular conditions do not define who I am. I am God expressed in individual being. My Source is God and my destiny is God. I know that these circumstances are here and I will pray that I may see how they can teach me. But in and of themselves the circumstances have no power to define Who I am.

When dealing with feelings of not-belonging, of being excluded or neglected, I try to reach for the awareness that the following affirmation represents:

> *Through my Oneness with God I am one with all of His expressions*

> It is impossible to be excluded or neglected. I might feel that way, but it is not accurate. I can never be separate from my unity with Creation, in any of its forms.

The following is an example from my own experience. When I gave birth to our third child, and as labor grew

more and more intense, I kept before me these words
of the 23rd Psalm that I had memorized for that purpose:

> *"The Lord is my Shepherd; I shall want nothing;*
> *He makes me lie down in green pastures,*
> *and leads me beside the waters of peace"*

(Ps. 23:1-2)

It helped me divest any energy I was tempted to extend
to my interpretation of the situation. Instead, the song
called on me to rely only and totally on my Shepherd. It
did not take the pain away, but the situation was put into
the right perspective and the circumstances became
bearable.

I use the following affirmation whenever I feel
insecure:

> *Here I am Lord, use me*

It helps divert my attention away from my own insecurity.
It helps me see that I am in that particular situation
probably not just for my own little self, but to be a door
through which Spirit can flow to others. *Here I am Lord,
use me.* This is one of those affirmations that can be
used throughout a lifetime, without ever growing stale.

MINI-MORNING-MEDITATIONS

Still another way to use affirmations is in the early
morning when waking up. It takes some training,
admitted, but it will prove very worthwhile.

Try to fill the very first waking moment of the day
with a thought that raises you above the sound of the

alarm clock. The words you say to yourself at that very moment will carry you through the day, especially when you recall them again at intervals during the day. This effect is not something that is obvious right away. It is something that works over time, by repeating the practice over and over again. As stated earlier in several instances, what matters is the intent to connect with the Divine. Words alone do nothing for you if they do not represent a feeling, an awareness that is dawning and that the words help to make concrete for you.

After some time you will notice that it is helpful to start the day in this way. And this is why it works. At the moment of rising your conscious mind is almost as a page not yet written on. You can write your dedication at the top of the sheet and thus give the day ahead of you a new dimension. In that way the day will start on the right note, and you do not have to be afraid that your busy agenda will swallow you up, bones and all.

Keep several small affirmations at hand and the one that happens to pop into your mind when you wake up you take for that morning. Say the words to yourself and wait for the feeling behind the words to wash over you. This may take only a few seconds, since your mind is not yet cluttered with trivial matters. Then get out of bed and go about your business. See if any of the following examples appeal to you:

> *I am one with Life*

> *Spirit is the essence of my being*

> *I am as God created me*

("A Course in Miracles")

> *This is the day the Lord has made, let us rejoice
> and be glad*

(Ps. 118:24)

I particularly love the last one. It gives a bounce to my
day. It states that this is the Lord's day, not mine. And to
rejoice and be glad about it means that it must be a terrific
day.   Why else bother rejoicing?   So, how can I have a
bad day? *I* cannot even *have* a day; neither a bad one nor
a good one. What I *can* have is a limited perspective, a
false sense   of self, that causes me to identify   with
occurrences and circumstances. This is the day the Lord
has made, and all His days are new and fresh. I would not
want to waste His day with my own little issues. So, I lift
up my head and become part of His day. Part of Life.

APPLICATION

Meditation is the key that opens the door to let the Light shine in. Like a map, an affirmation helps you locate that key. Whether you use affirmations in meditation, on the spot or in the early morning, they help remember who you are and what your life really is about.

A constant and consistent effort is necessary for reaping the benefits of meditation. It does not have to become a time consuming ritual. Better practiced meditation two or three times a day for only a few minutes, than once a week for an hour. Do not despair. It takes time to get used to turning body and mind in the direction of the Light. "In patience possess ye your soul", which in this respect means as much as: While intending to learn to meditate and waiting for meditation to become integrated into your life, you meet yourself. And that is, in part, what meditation is about.

1. Think about your individual spiritual ideal. Let the meaning behind the words wash over you. Can you think of a way to capture the essence of your spiritual ideal in an affirmation, just as the examples in this chapter show?

2. Is there a sample affirmation in this chapter that you would like to try out at your meditation time? If there is, write it down. Also, try to think of statements you remember hearing or reading that you could use in this way. It could be just a sentence, or part of a poem or a prayer. Write those down, too.

3. Affirmations on the spot. Think about a recurring difficult situation in your life. It could be a problem in the relationship with your child, or a child rearing issue that troubles you. It could be the end of the day blues from which many moms suffer, or the daily encounter with your children's friends.

   Whatever the issue, think of a short phrase, like the ones mentioned, that would help you re-focus your energy right then and there. Write down the one you come up with or copy an example you like.

   "Program" yourself to think this affirmation the minute you feel uneasy. Do not say or do anything until you feel you have regained composure.

   Although miracles are not excluded, do not be disappointed if you do not see one right away. This is a trial and error process, and it takes time and effort. Write down one or more affirmations on the spot you would like to try out.

4. Experiment with a mini-morning-meditation. It just takes a few seconds, so freeing up the time cannot be a problem. You might want to post a little note next to your alarm clock to help you remember. Think of a few words that capture a thought with which you would like to start the day, and write them down. Of course, you could also use one of the examples in this chapter.

   After a while, expand this practice by repeating the mini-morning-meditation statement several times during the day. For instance, you could agree that every time you wash your hands, or with every diaper change, you pause for a moment to say the statement in thought, try to feel its meaning, and then continue with what you are doing.

7

INNER GUIDANCE

I stand at the door and knock

-

Knock, and the door will be opened

The Christ

Now that we have taken an in-depth look at the development of inner life through meditation and prayer, we can look at yet another spiritual tool, namely inner guidance. Where prayer is the brush that cleans the room and meditation the key that opens the door, inner guidance is a lens. Inner guidance is a two-function lens that first focuses on helpful information within, and then projects that information as a beam of light onto the issue at hand.

CONSULTING INNER GUIDANCE

You might suppose that receiving inner guidance is something reserved for the holy, if not happy, few. Or that a special code or secret routine is necessary. On the contrary. Everyone always has access to inner guidance, no matter where they are and what they do. It is just that by cluttering up the mind with trivial matters and by failing to clarify priorities people do not see the message.

Fortunately you can actively do a few things to help yourself receive knowledge that comes from within. Four conditions form the basis for understanding inner guidance, and meeting them lies within the capabilities of all who are interested. They are: *expectancy* (or openness, or faith), *true need*, *careful preparation* and a *pure, simple question*.

Expectancy

Just as the wish is the father of the thought, so is expectancy the mother of receiving guidance. It is unlikely that you will recognize inner guidance if you do not hope for it and expect it to come. The key is to expect an answer, to trust and know that an answer will be given. Also, you need to let go of the preferred resolution you imagined. Expectancy is open, it cannot be pinned down to a specific outcome.

True need

It is reassuring to know that if there is a true need, if you really, really need to know, somehow you will be told. Seek and you will find, ask and you will receive, knock and the door will be opened. The way the answer appears may vary. It can come during meditation or right after, it can come as a thought, a feeling or an impression. It can come in a dream. It can come through people we interact with, without them even knowing it.

Careful preparation

You have to know with what you are dealing. Only then does the guidance you receive make any sense. Inner guidance is like a piece of a puzzle you receive. You cannot do a thing with a mere piece. Only when you have laid the groundwork, do you know where a new piece will fit and only then will it be helpful.

Pure, simple question

This requirement will help double fold. First, it forces you to become organized and figure out exactly what your question is. This takes pondering and reflection. A pure simple question is the result of a focused mind.

Second, when you do receive your message there is no room for doubt. It has to pertain to the one simple question you posed, and not to any one of a tangle of thoughts.

The following example of inner guidance comes from my own experience. I relate it here because it is an example of inner guidance, through a dream, where the four points just mentioned are clearly present. At the time when this occurred I had been having serious doubts about the sanity of exploring and assimilating metaphysical, esoteric and new age material. Edgar Cayce's ideas spoke to me particularly, and they had propelled me on a radical, adventurous path. I was very eager to continue to do research and to be enlightened, but I was not sure if all this new stuff was right for me. My perspective on life had been shifting notably. Had I gone crazy, or was I basically still the same old, though renewed, me? I simply *had* to know. I decided to plainly ask this question at the close of my evening meditation, urgently expecting an answer.   I had   no idea in what form the answer would come. That night, I had this dream:

"A new furnace is being installed in my home. A technician turns it on and shows me several digital thermometers that indicate the temperature at various points around the house. There even is a thermometer that shows the temperature of the incoming, outside air (-26°F!). The furnace runs smoothly, the house is nice and warm."

This dream was so vivid, it woke me up in the middle of the night. I was wide awake! It needed no explaining; I had no doubt what it meant. I was elated!

From this incident of inner guidance I learned a few things. First of all I learned to recognize and fully trust the "sound" of my inner voice. There was no doubt in my mind about the sincerity of the message, nor about its meaning. Moreover, I realized that the main reason for receiving and understanding it was the urgency of my need (*true need*) and my readiness to accept an answer (*expectancy*). I simply had to know, and this urgency felt very legitimate to me at the time. Also, I had done my homework. After careful consideration and contemplation I had had to conclude that the religious beliefs and customs of the church of my upbringing did not fit me (*preparation*). And after studying and assimilating these new concepts (the new furnace) for about a year at that time, I understood that once I would enter the path, there would come a point of no return. That explains the urgency I felt about the matter. Next, the question I asked, "Am I doing the right thing?", was a pure question, undiluted by ego-wishes, or unspoken messages, etc. It welled up from within, and in its simplicity spilled out (*pure, simple question*). And to round out the circle, the answer was short and clear: the house (me) is warm.

Another example of inner guidance in my own life is the time I could not find my keys. Like most mothers I have a substantial collection of keys, all on one ring. The keys to the various locks of the doors of the house, keys to both our cars and the garage door, the key to a friend's house, the key to the office at work, etc. That key ring is essential to the smooth running of my life. And now it was gone! I knew that it had to be somewhere in the house, for I had just returned home with the car. I questioned the kids, 4 and 2 at the time, but they were busy doing their own thing and keys did not interest them. After frantically searching the house for a while, looking in all the obvious places, I realized that panicking was not the way to find them. I decided to mentally step outside the situation for an instant. So I went to my room, closed the door and concentrated on my "center", as I like to call it. I told myself that if I really needed those keys, then somehow I would have them. Simply out of pure necessity, not by looking for them. I ordered myself to take my mind off the keys. After a few minutes I had calmed myself and went back to the kids in the family room. Without giving it a thought I walked over to the video cabinet, opened the doors ..... and there my keys were! It turned out that my two year old had gotten hold of them and tucked them away neatly and quietly.

If not for the decision to detach myself from the situation and call upon my inner being, it might have taken me all day to retrieve the keys.

Every day, parents are confronted with problems big and small. They face decisions of all kinds on a continual basis. Inner guidance is a must! Especially when dealing with children, whose reasoning abilities are only just budding. As a parent, you cannot always rely on your own experience from childhood, or on what "the books" say, or on the opinion of others. There are times when an issue can only be met with an authentic, original response, a response that can only come from within.

When problem situations arise, turn within and call upon your inner guidance and ask for God's will to be done. The following is the way you can make receiving inner guidance a part of your life. When an issue facing your child or facing you both, is really giving you a hard time, and you do not see a way out, then at your quiet time put the whole bag on the altar. In prayer empty yourself and divest any preference in outcome and place the issue, the child and yourself in the hands of Life. Then pray that on the right moment you may be shown or told what to do. When the feeling of total trust washes over you, you know that God's will is going to be done. Then deliberately put the whole issue aside. You might have to repeat this several days in a row, until a solution is found, or a decision made. It could also happen that your perspective changes and the issue stops bothering you. Because the change can come on the inside as well. It is truly amazing to witness Inner Direction take over. Consulting your inner guidance is the key to this occurrence.

As you may have guessed, receiving inner guidance, prayer and meditation (lens, brush and key) are very much connected. They are not isolated practices. The tools are best used together. They overlap, support and reinforce each other, until they have become so much a part of your life that you do no longer distinguish one from the other.

DREAMS

Dreams are yet another way of receiving information from beyond our physical reality, as the earlier example of the furnace dream shows. The Bible contains many examples where dreams guide and help people on their life's path. The book of Genesis tells the story of Joseph (the great-grandson of Abraham) who was put in prison in Egypt.

> *One night the Pharaoh of Egypt has two puzzling dreams, but there is no one who can interpret them for him. The Pharaoh's butler then remembers Joseph in the dungeon who can interpret dreams. Joseph is summoned to appear before the Pharaoh. After hearing the explanation of his dreams, the Pharaoh is much relieved. He makes Joseph ruler over Egypt, to enact the measures called for by the message in the dreams.*

(adapted from Genesis 41)

And yet another example, this time from the Bible's New Testament:

> *"After they [the three wise men] had gone, an angel of the Lord appeared to Joseph in a dream and said to him, 'Rise up, take the child and his mother and escape with them to Egypt, and stay there until I tell you; for Herod is going to search for the child to do away with him.' So Joseph rose from sleep, and taking mother and child by night he went away with them to Egypt, and there he stayed till Herod's death."*

(Mt:13-15)

It is noteworthy that the subjects in these two stories have no doubt whatsoever concerning the authenticity of the message in their dreams, nor do hesitate to act on that message. I have heard it said that a dream not studied is like a letter from God unopened. The avenue of inner guidance through dreams is always open to all.

Dream study is a very exciting field, worthy of your time and attention. As with any study that is worthwhile, to truly benefit from it you have to commit to a continuous, daily effort. If dream study appeals to you, begin with getting informed about it. Your library surely has a few volumes on dream study that can help you get started.

I have to admit, however, that in my experience dream study sometimes demanded too much. It is extremely hard to be consistent in recording dreams upon awakening, let alone right after receiving them. Parents of young children savor every minute of undisturbed sleep, and it takes quite a leap of faith to program yourself to wake up after receiving a dream. Also, many times the first sounds in the morning come from a child. No time to write anything down! The period I did manage to study my dreams brought me at least one important insight though: dreams come to help. No matter how funny, weird or scary they may be, they always come to help.

The following is an example of a dream I had one night. It proved to me that dreams can shed much needed light on issues facing me. In the days prior to the dream I had considered engaging myself in a "new age" activity that was taking place in the area where I was living at the time. I was curious and eager to get involved. At the same time I felt a little uneasy and was not sure where that feeling was trying to lead me. Before I relate the dream here, I need to explain that in working with my dreams I had been able to identify my   children appearing in my dreams as symbols for my developing spiritual   life.   Water   and   fish   are both well-known symbols for spiritual life and food. The dream went as follows:

"One of my children and I are in a small boat on a lake. He moves his arms about in the water, stirring up the sand and sediment. The water turns turbid. I start to fish, but the fish I pull up are dead."

Needless to say, I abandoned my plans right away. Once more I was reminded to heed the small voice warning me for trouble.

Every night, a celestial messenger delivers a bundle of letters to the doorstep of the conscious mind. There is no obligation to pick them up and read them. But of one thing you can be sure: dreams come to help. Funny dreams and serious dreams, scary, haunting and repeating dreams, they   all come   to be· of assistance.   They give explanations and insights, they warn or remind you and they balance your life.

STILL NOT SURE?

Suppose you want to make a certain decision, but you are not sure whether this decision is in harmony with your ideals or not. Is this the decision that is most helpful to you and the people around you? You pray, you meditate, ask for guidance, you listen..., but still you are not sure. How can you find out if this is the right thing for you to do or not at this point in time?

When this happens, it is good to remember that we learn by doing. A child that crawls will not learn to walk by thinking about it, or by watching other people walk. It needs to pull herself up at the table and stand on her own legs as an indication of her resolve to learn to walk. Only then will a parent be able to take that child by the hand and lead her.

So it is with us when learning to walk the spiritual path. Only when we are willing to lift ourselves up and take the risk of falling down, will the Creative Forces be able to steer us. A boat that is puttering along can be turned around and sent in a new, and even opposite, direction. But when the motor is not on, there is not much that the rudder can do. We learn by doing; we learn by applying all that we know.

This chapter on inner guidance completes the section of the book dealing with inner life and turning within. Besides the all important tool called the spiritual ideal (your compass), you have assembled a few more instruments to put into your toolbox: a brush, a key, instructions for use and a two-way lens (prayer, meditation, affirmations and inner guidance).

The last three chapters of this book deal with the practical application of spirituality. You will see how these tools (and a couple more) perform in day to day life with kids.

APPLICATION

1. Can you recall an instance when you received inner guidance that was helpful and that you used successfully?

2. Is there an issue in your life on which you would like to get a new perspective? It needs to be something that really concerns you and really touches you (*true need*). Did you inform yourself about it as much as you could? Did you fit together as many pieces of the puzzle as you possibly could (*careful preparation*)? In a few words write down the issue on which you would like to receive inner guidance.

3. Release. You need to let go of the anxiety about the matter. Expectancy presupposes an openness to accept a new way of looking at things. Anxiety is caused by imagining a negative outcome. Prayer can help to release those worrying images.
   Imagery can help in this respect, too. Close your eyes and visualize a basket in front of you. Put your issue in this basket, including your anxiety and your preferred resolution. Search and identify all remaining feelings and worries and place them in the basket one by one, until there is nothing left. Imagine a colorful ribbon wrapped around the basket, tied in a bow on top. You do not need it any more, so send it away. Send it to Mother Earth, or to Father Sky. They will surely find a way to transform your packet into something useful, somewhere, sometime. Imagine the basket with its bow floating up and away, growing smaller and smaller, until it disappears from sight. If this kind of exercise

appeals to you, you might benefit from repeating it on following days. When you really feel relieved from worry, you are ready to accept an answer that comes from within (*expectancy*).

4. It seems contradictory, but at the same time that you are working on release of anxiety, you will need to pinpoint where exactly you need an extra puzzle piece. Consider the matter "detached", not emotionally involved. Formulate your question in a short sentence that can be answered with "yes" or "no."

    Phrasing your question this way will make it easier to understand the inner guidance you receive (*pure, simple question*). Specific expectations about the answer can block the road to you, and you will not see the answer. Also, you do not know yet in what form the answer will come. It can come in a variety of ways, so do not focus on only one possible form.

5. Dreams. To get a feel for what dreams can tell you, you would need to write down dreams on a regular basis. That way you will get acquainted with the "stuff" your dreams are made of. You will get familiar with your own symbols and images. Do you think this is the right time to embark on dream study? If so, consult the bibliography and of course your local library. Once you decide on an approach you feel comfortable with, stay with it for a while, before you add new perspectives. It is easy to get lost in this field, or to overfeed yourself. If you think that this is not the right time for you to work with dreams, do not feel bad. At a later time you might want to make the effort. Or maybe dreams are simply not your cup of tea. That is fine, too.

8

PRACTICAL SPIRITUALITY

Put into practice day by day that as is known.
Not some great deed or act, or speech,
but line upon line, precept upon precept,
here a little, there a little

Edgar Cayce

PERSPECTIVES ON PRACTICAL SPIRITUALITY

Before going on a tour of a variety of parenting issues
to see how spiritual concepts can be brought to bear on
them, let's first look at three perspectives that allow you to
apply spirituality in everyday life. These three perspectives
are:

– Looking for the message in each experience
– Turning stumbling blocks into stepping stones
– Making choices in the right spirit

These three perspectives are like frames or molds. They
are the tools that help you see your situation in a new way,
and they encourage you to apply what you know to be true

spiritually. The first two perspectives have to do with your interaction with the outside world. The third frame, making choices in the right spirit, challenges you to turn within and find there what is true.

LOOKING FOR THE MESSAGE IN EACH EXPERIENCE

True happiness does not come from the things of the world. Happiness is found within. But you still need the outside world. You need it to apply what you know and to test yourself. You need it to try out new ways, to make mistakes, to learn and to grow. Being in the world in a sense resembles being in school. Subjects are presented, lessons are learned, you interact with teachers and fellow students, you goof now and then, and you succeed now and then.

This image of life as a school can be very helpful. All that you experience becomes a learning experience. Once a lesson is learned, new material is presented. The people around you are students of Life as well. The contents of their lessons may be very different, even if they live their lives right next to you. The classes are all mixed up, so to speak, but the end goal for all is the same: to be one with God and to love your neighbor as yourself.

The things that happen to you, the people and things you get involved in are all opportunities to learn and to grow. Experiences can be very painful, especially when they seem to repeat themselves. But each and every experience in your life has something to teach you. In a sense, every experience is a message. You do not need to live through variations on a theme that is painful, if you are open and receptive to the message that the experience holds for you. If you are willing to act on that message, hurtful experiences do not need to repeat themselves.

It is tempting to consider an occurrence only at its face value. It often seems so obvious that certain causes make an occurrence inevitable. You can always point to other people, or to yourself, and determine who was at fault. Sadly these paths only lead backward, to causes and mistakes that lie in the past. Beyond the appearance of cause and effect there is the promise of a purpose in every experience. Looking through the obvious threads of causality you will find new hope. Instead of struggling through an experience and resisting its message and implications, you can open yourself to the message. When you open yourself to the message an experience holds for you, you will see new ways to go. It is not an easy task, but "armed" with a prayerful attitude, and with your individual spiritual ideal clearly in mind, the lessons of your experiences will become clear. And when you are able to integrate the newly found insights into your consciousness, you can move on to an ever more fulfilling life.

Being a parent is one such experience that offers a spectrum of messages and lessons. Although there are lessons that generally all parents need to learn, each parent has her or his own curriculum. Each parent has to decide for herself or himself what exactly it is that she or he needs to receive.

To begin to get a feel for the message that an experience is presenting you with, it is absolutely essential to look at yourself and at what is happening from an "ego detached" perspective. It is impossible to gain any kind of spiritual insight if you are personally caught up in a situation. What enables you to let go of your ego centered perspective is to reach for the spiritual perspective. By applying and living your spiritual ideal you base your life on Spirit, which lies beyond the realm of the ego. Through prayer, meditation and contemplation you will receive the strength and insight to face any circumstance and look for the message it holds for you.

TURNING STUMBLING BLOCKS INTO STEPPING STONES

Although your life from now on has a sound foundation in your spiritual ideal, this does not mean that your life will run along smoothly. Obstacles and problems will still arise and you will be very much involved in working these out. But your perspective has changed dramatically. Even though an obstacle will remain an obstacle, it is no longer debilitating. Although a problem will still demand your full attention, now you will look for solutions to come from a different direction, namely from within.

Problems and obstacles occur in all aspects of life: family, health, work, finances, etc. Not all problems have a ready solution. Some need to be worked with and accepted for a lifetime. Problems may be personal, family or group related. Some are major difficulties that throw you into despair, and others are minor, but nonetheless nagging. Whatever the obstacle you bump into, make sure you recognize what exactly is going on: you were running along smoothly and now this is bothering you. Or you have never really been able to take off because a certain matter is keeping you from doing so. Recognize what it is you want to do, and what it is that is keeping you from doing it. Psychologists and other problem solving specialists assure us that this is the preliminary step to any kind of progress in a situation: become aware of what is going on. Clearly this is not always easy to do. You have an image of yourself and from this perspective the association with a certain problem might not fit that image. If you have a major obstacle in an area of your life, it can be very helpful to read and get informed about the issue. There is nothing better than to know where you stand and what your options are.

However, a new dimension to the conventional problem solving techniques opens up when you relate your life's problems to your spiritual ideal. You now have a consciously chosen set of ideals, based on your one spiritual ideal. When you start to apply the practical steps you devised yourself, you will begin to integrate the spiritual ideal, and the ideals flowing from it, into your mind set, into your world of reference, into your framework of priorities. Over a period of time, this will result in a different outlook on life and life's happenings.

You might discover that with this new perspective the old problem does not bother you so much any more. Or you might discover a different angle from which to approach it. You might even find a way to directly apply your spiritual ideal to this issue. If indecision or hesitation has been part of your difficulty, you will now feel a new resolve, a clearer sense of direction that enables you to take bold steps. But most of all, viewing life and life's stumbling blocks from a spiritual perspective enables you to look through the appearance and see in its place a stepping stone. Consider the following analogy:

You are taking a hike on a mountain trail. While looking ahead to where you are going, you trip on a rock, fall and hurt yourself.

Now there are several options. You could get up, get tough and make yourself a crutch from a piece of wood, and continue. You could take a break, nurse your foot and continue on your way later, when you feel better. You could call for help and continue with assistance. You could get angry and start kicking the rock with your good foot.

Yet another way to respond would be to see this tripping rock as a stone to stand on. You step on it, injured as you may be, and from atop the rock you have a higher lookout point. You now discover that further down to the left there is a shortcut. Or you might see a path to the right that you would much rather take in view of your recently discovered ideals. And even if you remain committed to the old road, accepting the rock as part of the trail enables you to gain a broader perspective. With renewed motivation you jump off, forget the pain and continue on your way.

Of course, analogies are never perfect, and this one is no exception. Hopefully it makes clear to you the concept of making a stumbling block into a stepping stone. The main idea is not to get hung up on the obstacle as something to stumble over. Accept the situation as it is. Acknowledge feelings of anger, frustration, irritation, disappointment or resentment. But do not get stuck in those feelings. Once you have felt and acknowledged them, allow yourself to move beyond those feelings. Mentally step outside the situation for a moment and think to yourself:

All that matters is being a channel for Life, making my will one with God's. So, Creation, here I am, I offer you this situation that, from my perspective, looks like an impasse, a dead end. I offer it to you, knowing that you will see new answers, new possibilities. I offer myself as well. Here I am Lord, your child is listening.

Then do not let it bother you any more. Go about your business as best as you can and as joyfully as you can. A way *will* be shown. Be open and expectant. Simply *assume* that things will work out for the best. And they will.

MAKING CHOICES IN THE RIGHT SPIRIT

Making choices is part of life. You make choices all the time. You make small choices, like where to buy food, what to wear, whether to take a hike or ride a bike, etc. Small, daily choices that are not that significant but ones through which you can express who you are. You make important choices as well. You choose the people with whom you associate, what kind of a home you live in, the way you spend leisure time, etc. Choices that really matter and that affect other people too. These choices are influenced by what you feel like at the moment, by what you have gotten used to, by what you assume to be morally just, or by what looks like a sensible thing to do, etc.

All choices you make have consequences. The small choices set in motion a pattern of consequences, that, although perhaps not far reaching, does help to determine the flow of your life. The important choices often have far reaching consequences. They affect not only yourself but others as well, and they influence you for longer periods of time, if not for the rest of your life. No wonder that at times you find yourself worrying that you might not make the right choice.

The determination whether a choice is good or bad, right or wrong, depends on your perspective, it depends on your point of view. And it may be clear that there is hardly any constancy in that. What may look like the right choice now, appears to have been the wrong one later. What may seem a good choice to some, looks like a bad one to others.

There clearly is a need for a different measuring instrument to determine the basis for making decisions. A measuring instrument that lifts you above the web of opposing arguments. Beyond the level of apparent right and wrong choices lies the level of the underlying spirit. Right and wrong choices as such do not exist. What *does* exist is the right spirit in which to make a choice.

This may sound strange at first. It sounds as if there is no objective way to analyze options and weigh them rationally. But there is. Only now the level on which the objective analysis and rational weighing of options take place is a deeper one. The right spirit in which to make a choice refers to the underlying intent. The right spirit behind a choice has to do with who you really are.

What then, is the right spirit in which to make a choice? How will you know if you are being inspired by the right spirit? How do you identify the spirit that is right for you individually, on which to base your choices? These questions lead directly to your individual spiritual ideal.

Your target of ideals is a tool, that enables you to weigh matters in a way that makes sense to you. You hold the options you have right up next to the target of ideals and you will discover which arguments truly speak to you and your situation, and which do not. If you like you can devote a section of the target to the matter. In your stated ideals you might even find a motive or intent that you had not yet brought to the issue at hand. Remember that you yourself were the one who designed the contents of the ideals; they reflect *your* inner truth. What better tool can you find with which to "crack" your life's issues? It is an authentic, individual manner to tackle any decision, and it needs no outside justification. When an honest assessment takes place, when you weigh the arguments of both sides against your inner sense of truth and purpose (pros and cons placed next to your ideals), then you know that the choice you make is the right one for you. Because the spirit in which you make it is the right one.

Parents face choices and decisions all the time. What they decide affects not only them but their children as well. Often, finding a solution that offers a place to every family member's needs and priorities feels like looking for a five-legged lamb! But a solution that works for all need not be so hard to come by. You now have a spiritual toolbox with some very useful instruments: Your spiritual ideal and a choice of spiritual practices, namely prayer, meditation and consulting inner guidance. Let's look at an example to see how you can work with these tools in everyday life:

Nicole's class is preparing a parent night. The children are rehearsing a small play that they will perform on the stage in the school cafeteria. In addition each child has made an art project to present to their parents on parent night. Nicole is very excited and eager to show her parents the work she has been doing. But it just so happens that parent night is scheduled on the same night Nicole's mother had agreed to co-host the annual fundraising dinner and auction of the town's museum. Nicole's mother is in a bind. She wants to be at the school's parent night to be with her daughter, as well as fulfill her commitment at the museum. Clearly, she cannot be in two places at the same time. She needs to make a choice.

Depending on her spiritual ideal and the mental and physical ideals flowing from it, she is sure to find a solution that works for all involved. Suppose Carol from the example in Chapter 2 faces this dilemma. Her spiritual ideal is *Guide children,* and her mental ideal relating to this issue is *Practice patience and tolerance.* She discusses the matter with her husband, who will be attending the school night, and with her daughter Nicole. She takes the time to consult her inner guidance. While keeping her ideals firmly in mind, Carol comes up with the following: She will come to school during the day and help the children prepare for the evening's performance. Her husband will video-tape the play. And on the next night she and Nicole will view the tape together and Nicole will then present her mother with her gift. On Carol's next activity at the museum, inspecting and making an inventory of stored items, she will bring along Nicole to help. The input Carol receives from her husband and daughter when making this proposal, will help her decide to either follow this scenario, or to look for another solution (e.g., finding a way to leave the museum fund-raiser for a while so as to be present a the parent night for at least some of the time.)

A parent with a different set of ideals will come up with a different solution. If the spiritual ideal is *Be an innovator* with the mental ideal *Make time to have fun together,* the solution might be to see the dilemma as an opportunity to introduce the children to the local museum. The parent decides to invite the class over for a workshop at the museum, to introduce the kids to new concepts and to broaden their horizon, in keeping with the parent's spiritual ideal of innovation. Although he will not attend the parent night at school, he found a way to connect his child's life with his own.

When faced with choices and dilemmas, open yourself to the wisdom from within by calling upon inner guidance. When you truly connect with your spiritual intent and feel its value, feel its quality, and are willing to let go of any preconceived ideas or imagined solutions, you are sure to resolve the issue in a way that is best for all concerned.

APPLICATION

1. Each experience holds a *message*. When things run along smoothly you do not tend to think in terms of messages and lessons in occurrences and experiences. You can get away with enjoying yourself without having to probe very deeply. However, when obstacles arise, when things do not run smoothly, that's when you really need to involve yourself consciously. Then you need to ask some investigative questions like: "How can I change my attitude or perspective?", "What do I need to release?", "Are my priorities clear and do I live them consistently?", etc. The spiritual practices of prayer, meditation and asking for inner guidance will help you focus on which questions to ask. To help you think along this line, try to identify an event that, although painful or traumatic, proved to be an experience through which you learned and gained wisdom. Example:

    > A person's hurtful comment on your involvement in a project makes you become aware of your priorities. Thus the painful experience has strengthened your resolve to stay committed.

2. Can you imagine an example where a *stumbling block* can turn into a *stepping stone*? Just think of an ordinary problem (like not having the car on Fridays) and how you can turn it around into something constructive (like taking the kids for a stroll or bike ride; inviting friends over). To practice your resourcefulness, imagine a few of these kinds of situations.

3. At this moment do you face an important *choice*? Consider devoting a section of your ideals target to this issue. Remember that your spiritual ideal represents your own individual sense of truth and purpose in life. It holds the key to a decision that expresses what you stand for. And only with a decision like that can you be at peace.

Refer to the steps in Chapter 2. Some of the personal qualities that do not appear in the wording of your spiritual ideal might help you. Read the section on mental and physical ideals again to help you in the process of phrasing ideals. When you have found words for the attitude that fits your spiritual ideal and thereby you, you have already found an indication of the direction of the physical steps that you want to take. Make sure that you feel at peace with the formulation of both the spiritual ideal and the mental ideal. If they truly represent who you are, practical steps that work for all involved are guaranteed to become clear to you. Your sincere intent to find a solution that benefits all involved, is what will carry you through this process.

9

USING SPIRITUAL TOOLS IN
DAILY LIFE WITH KIDS

*For it is in the application, not the knowledge,
that the truth becomes a part of you*

Edgar Cayce

Now you are ready to look for ways to integrate the newly found insights. You are aware of spiritual realities that previously lay hidden from your view, and you can determine what changes this new awareness is challenging you to make in your daily life. In addition to becoming familiar with a variety of tools, like the setting of ideals, prayer, meditation and consulting inner guidance, you have gained three new perspectives on practical spirituality. Now it is time to put all your tools together in your toolbox. The combined and alternated use of the tools in your box will allow you to brave all the storms parenthood may have in store for you. The following sections deal with some issues that come up almost daily in family life.

They are:

disagreements	children's questions
sibling fights	TV
illness	wanting the best for your child
balancing needs	anger
children's demands	discipline

Anger and discipline will be discussed in the next chapter. You will learn how to relate each of these issues to spiritual concepts. And most importantly, you will see how you can use the spiritual tools you have assembled to meet the challenges these issues pose.

DISAGREEMENTS

There will be times when you and your child do not agree. If you yourself possess a degree of tenacity or stubbornness, chances are your child will too. But even without a clearly visible shared strong will feature, children at times show an urgent desire to be independent. Or to put it simple, they want to have things their way. Since this is not always possible or desirable, disagreements are bound to arise. The topic can vary from the choice of clothing or food to the amount of time spent watching TV, or more seriously, homework and the choice of friends.

Learning strategies to survive storms concerning these matters can be helpful to get a fresh perspective. What matters even more though, is to find a way to deal with disagreements that is in sync with your newly discovered ideals. But how can spirituality be practical when you find yourself right in the middle of an earsplitting uproar? Well, as soon as you realize that things are out of control, you stop. The well-known cure for anger, "slowly count to 10", is not too far off the mark. You mentally step outside the situation for a moment. You divest yourself completely from the way this communication is conducted. The first result of this divesting will be that you notice that for the main part your child has been reacting to your strong opinion on the matter. When you let go, there is less need for the child to have a strong, opposing, opinion also. By your renunciation of fighting, you have cleared the table on the physical level. It is the first thing needed to prepare for spiritual reality to become apparent.

Now, turn within. Center yourself and divest any personal preference for outcome. Empty yourself of any favored resolution, thereby clearing the table on the mental level. Pray that you may be a channel Life, a tool for Life to do with Life (the child) what it intends to do. Now the spiritual reality becomes apparent. Your child is a child of Life, just as you are. The child has been entrusted to your care for a period of time, but the child is not yours, she is Life's child. The child has come here for a purpose. Life has an agenda for the child. Sense within you a total trust in Life to do that which is right for all concerned. Only then will there be room in you for Life to move through you. And Life will. Exit frustration and anger, enter release and calm. At this point it is easy to feel the love you have for your child well up inside you. From a worried and opinionated parent you have turned into a fellow-traveler on the path of Life. Now you are open to perceive a solution that works for all involved.

It takes practice and anticipation to respond in an alternative way like this. You might want to prepare a short affirmation ahead of time, so that when times get really hectic, it will pop up right before you and help you reconsider. You will see that it works for your benefit as well as your child's. Moreover, you will discover that you can use the same process in relation to other people as well.

SIBLING FIGHTS

You can believe me if I tell you that, as the youngest of four, I was involved in many a fight when growing up. Now, as a mother of three boys, ages 12, 10 and 8, I witness at least as many.

When my children fight it looks as if they are picking a fight on purpose, just to tease or nag each other. Sometimes it feels that they are out to get me, the parent, because they know fighting upsets me. The appearance is definitely one of annoyance, of disturbance that I would like to get rid of as soon as possible. When I take the time to probe one layer deeper though, to the mental level, a new perspective opens up. Looking at fighting from a mental perspective I discover that the kids are testing new abilities and new insights. Another possibility is that the children are trying to find a way to reach a fair balance of give and take in their relationship.

Not all fighting among siblings is necessarily destructive. You should not let yourself get upset at each and every loud exchange that your kids may have, and make an end to their communication right then and there. Try to determine what exactly is going on. Is it honing of skills and balancing of positions? Or is one child abusing the other and deliberately trying to dominate the other child and force her will on him? It takes an experienced eye to distinguish among these possibilities. Of course if the last scenario is taking place you need to step in and protect the child that is taken advantage of, as well as investigate the causes of the first child's dominating behavior. In her many books Swiss psychologist Alice Miller points out that children re-enact to others what has been done to them. Thinking along this line certainly puts the parents on the spot. Watching your children quarrel and fight might give you some clues as to the quality of your own and other adults' communication skills in relation to your children.

In addition, there is a spiritual way to look at quarrels and fights. On some deep level your children have chosen to be together. They each have a role to play in the life of the other. Whether they punch or play, deep down they know there is a connection between them. It just takes a lot of playing and punching to find the right expression for that connection.

There is something else kids learn from quarrels and fights, and that is that hating and hitting do not have the last word in their relationship. Friendship and loyalty do. Only when they have lived through disharmony and disagreement can they truly appreciate the value of genuine friendship and loyalty. All this does not go to say that fighting is always okay and that all will work out for the best. No. You need to develop a keen eye to see what exactly is occurring.

Also, you can guide your children to learn to take responsibility for their words and actions. After all, it is their relationship, and in the end they are responsible for the quality of that relationship. Ask for their analysis and suggestions to improve the quality of communication. If you need more information on this subject of teaching children to take responsibility for their actions, consult the bibliography and of course your library.

Arguments and fights are such physical expressions of children's inner experiences that it is hard to look beyond the appearance offered by your eyes and ears. But even in this case, knowledge of the spiritual reality beyond the physical appearance, if not relieve your anxiety, at least will give you a broader perspective and a steadier beat of your heart.

ILLNESS

Few images rend the heart as does the image of a suffering child. The apparent injustice is striking, and you wonder how a supreme being could tolerate an innocent child to suffer. Feelings of frustration, anger and powerlessness overtake, and doubts arise about the sanity of Life and of Creation. We want to forcefully eradicate illness and suffering from our children's and all children's lives. But this we cannot. We face the seemingly impossible task to live with illness and suffering and not lose courage.

Jesus in his day saw a lot of sick and suffering people. His first reaction always was to relieve pain, to heal the sick and to restore the physical body to its perfect condition. On many occasions he connected healing with the forgiving of sins and with faith. You might wonder if you would qualify to be healed, if you have enough faith and are worthy to have your sins forgiven. But what is "faith" other than the willingness to let go of your ego-centered outlook on life and to reach for spiritual reality? And what is "being forgiven of sins" other than recognizing your true identity as a perfect child of God, as a child of Life? It is not a matter of qualifying or not, of being worthy or not. It is a matter of consciously letting God, Life, enter into your life. For Life all things are possible.

We are not the first ones to feel frustration in the face of suffering. At one point Jesus' students ask him why a man was born blind (John 9:1). They wondered if his blindness was related to his sins or to the sins of his parents. And Jesus answers: "He was born blind so that God's power might be displayed in curing him." And he cures the man. That is certainly an unexpected answer. He does not share in the students' frustration. He does not engage in a medical discussion, nor does he lay out a philosophy on the influence of diet, attitudes, karma, etc. on our health. He does not look back to causes, but he looks ahead, at what might happen next. And next, the man is cured.

When healing the sick, Jesus bypasses both the physical world with its ways and cures (pills, surgery, etc.), and the mental world with its ways and cures (karma, beliefs, etc.) Instantly, he perceives the spiritual reality and thus makes himself subject to the principles of the spiritual world. He looks beyond the appearance of a sick body to the true identity of his neighbor: a child of God, perfect as God created him. Jesus' spiritual perception of a person's condition overrules the physical perception the person has of himself, namely "I am sick." But only when he opens up to spiritual truth. When the man expresses the willingness to trust Life (faith) and to recognize his true origin as a perfect child of God (sins being forgiven), only then can he enter into Jesus' world of perfection and be healed.

Jesus holds out a prospect to his listeners that someday they will do the same works he does, and even more. But until that time we will have to deal with illness and suffering in the best way we know how, while learning the lessons the stumbling block of illness carries with it. How does "the best way we know how" translate into practical terms? We can let the spiritual ideal lead the way. It will provide us with an answer of integrity. Although the purpose or function of illness stays unclear and suffering remains an enigma, we can stay true to our conviction of truth in life in a practical manner, namely by applying our spiritual ideal.

If illness or suffering is a fact of life for you, include it in your target of ideals. Relating illness to your inner intent through the framework of ideals gives you a firm foundation in the face of questions and mysteries. You will be as effective as you can be, because through your honest and wholesome involvement you are connected to the matter at hand on all levels of your being: spiritually, mentally and physically.

APPLICATION

Illness

Having children means that rearing them and being with them is part of your life plan. Now that they are here, they form, at least in part, the reason why you are here. It may sound like logic taken backwards, but it is true all the same. If your child is sick or suffering, try to discover in what way and to which degree you need to be involved in your child's life. What does your involvement mean to the child and to yourself? Illness and suffering demand that you become clear about your priorities in life, and discover the way in which to express your commitment to your child in the best way.

Refer to the steps outlined for the setting of ideals. Think about attitudes and perspectives that flow from your spiritual ideal and that make sense concerning your issue. Then, conclude what concrete actions you can take to make the attitude and its spirit manifest in the physical world.

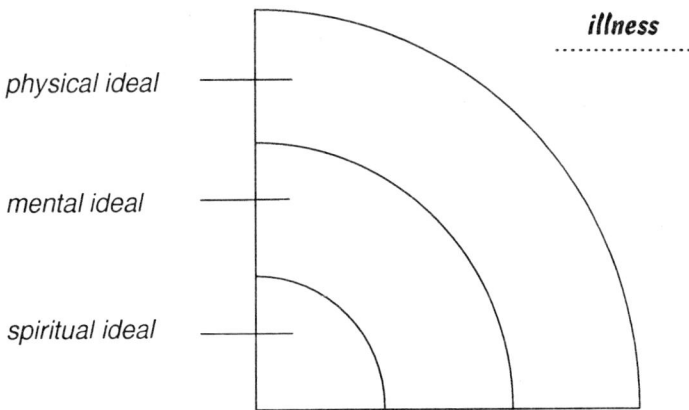

physical ideal

mental ideal

spiritual ideal

illness

Fig. 5

BALANCING NEEDS

Throughout the time you live together with your children you face the issue of balancing your children's needs and your own. Whether you are conscious of them or not, decisions are made daily. You are continuously weighing desires and needs, adjusting agendas and setting priorities.

Caring for your children is decidedly the most time consuming during their first five years of life. It follows that the issue of balancing needs and agendas comes most clearly into focus during this time. Mothers and fathers alike often feel that there is nothing left of their own agenda. Ever since the arrival of children, the parents' agenda has been determined for the main part by the needs of the children. Well, now that you have children, parenting is part of your life's purpose. Answering to the needs of your children has become part of your own agenda, and you will want to devote a big chunk of your time to them. But parents are individuals, too. Making time to express what you hold dearly, apart from your children, is of course justified. Once your youngest child enters kindergarten, she will start to have her own world. Then your physical involvement will diminish. But during the first five or six years, when children are still so very dependent physically as well as otherwise, balancing their needs with your own is like walking a tight rope.

An example of an area in which this tension of needs comes into the open, is the area of career versus home making. For quite some time a lively discussion has been going on in society about the pros and cons of both parents working versus one parent, or parents alternating, staying at home. Often these exchanges are marked by a judgmental attitude on the part of both sides towards the position of the other side. There is a sense that there is a right and a wrong way to decide this issue. Staying at home full time limits career possibilities, reduces disposable income and restricts societal contacts, and thus cannot be right. On the other hand, the argument goes, parents who both work do not dedicate enough time to the upbringing of their offspring and thus this cannot be right either. This is a no-win proposition. If you get caught in going back and forth between the various arguments of both camps in search of the right choice, you will end up frazzled and undecided.

Remember, right and wrong choices do not exist. What does exist is the right spirit in which to make a choice. This is true for the issue of career versus homemaking as it is for any other issue. Parents, each working with their own target of ideals, will come down on this issue differently. Although different choices result, each individual choice will be the right one for that particular parent. And that's because the choice is based on inner intent, on an individual spiritual ideal.

When you connect your intent to your actions, when you connect your heart to your hands, you will be at peace. During this process of linking intent with action, turning within is a must. It is all too easy to slip back into familiar attitudes and reactions that obstruct new insights that come from within. A prayerful attitude will help you to stay open and perceive solutions that might otherwise remain unnoticed.

CHILDREN'S DEMANDS

Parents sometimes envy their children. Children seem to have a boundless energy and they can be active for so long. Preschoolers, for instance, go about their playing and exploring in an unrestricted, all-out manner, and you wonder how they keep it up the entire day. And then, you might sometimes wonder how you yourself are going to keep it up till children's bed time. At times like this, when you feel exhausted and depleted, a child's demand or question can pull you over the edge and you respond in an irritated or angry manner. When a child is upset or hurt and comes to you for consolation, it sometimes feels you have nothing left to give; you have already given the child all you have.

Setting limits and house rules and enforcing them will help in this respect. But even if you are setting limits and enforcing them, your children's demands can sometimes be overwhelming. You wonder if they think you are inexhaustible. The truth is, that in a way they think you are. Children glorify their parents. They see in you the best that you can be. As far as children are concerned parents are the Source of all that they need. But parents themselves are not the Source. They are the window through which blessings may pass. Life uses parents as channels to give children what they need. "You are the bows from which your children as living arrows are sent forth" (Kahlil Gibran). When you are aware of this, it becomes a lot easier to give of yourself. Because then you know to give of your inner self that is connected to Life, and you can trust Life to supply you with what is needed. You are the channel through which God's Energy flows, bringing Life to both, your child and yourself. Let's look at this issue from another perspective. Imagine that your body does not actually stop where your skin ends, but that it extends beyond it in the form of an emanating energy field, or aura. Your own energy surrounds you, and an egg-like form, made of your own energy, encapsulates your physical body. When you talk to someone, or shake hands, then not only do you exchange words and a touch, but you exchange energy as well. Your aura and the other person's aura contact and exchange energy. A young child's energy field is not fully developed yet. Small children need to "refill" with strength every now and then through an adult who does have a fully developed energy field. That is why small children love to be on their parent's lap, or to hold hands. Because then they effectively are within the protection of the adult's energy field. In her book about healing and the aura Barbara Ann Brennan talks about the developing aura and the connection between the aura and the chakras, the physical contact points with Spirit Energy. She writes:

> "The field of the child is entirely open and vulnerable to the atmosphere in which he lives. ... The child's chakras are all open in the sense that there is no protective film over them which screens out the incoming psychic influences. This makes the child very vulnerable and impressionable. Thus, even though the chakras are not developed like those of an adult, and the energy that comes into them is experienced in a vague way, it still goes right into the field of the child, and the child must deal with it in some way. ... At around the age of seven, a protective screen is formed over the chakra openings that filters out a lot of the incoming influences from the universal energy

> *field. Thus, the child is no longer as vulnerable as before.*
> *This stage can be seen as a child grows and individuates.*
> *It is near the time of the dawning reason."*

"Hands of Light. A Guide to Healing Through the
Human Energy Field", by Barbara Ann Brennan

Part of your role as a parent is to be a channel of strength and reassurance to your child. The child, in turn, will learn by example and fulfill the role of giver of strength to other children, receiving the strength from his inner being. It is beautiful to see this happen.

Looking at it from a new perspective, your children's demands can form a wake up call. Connect to your inner being and give what the child needs, namely the strength and reassurance that can only come through your inner being, the true loaves and fishes. By doing so, you have turned the stumbling block of the unending need for parental support into a stepping stone. You have seized the opportunity and have connected to the Source.

This new attitude by no means requires you to give in every time a child expresses a need. Use your common sense and keep your educational objectives clearly in mind. When you have become used to expecting strength to come from within, inner guidance will come to your aid to decide in what way best to respond. You will know whether to strengthen the child with true food, or to encourage her to be self sufficient.

APPLICATION

Children's demands

1. Are you often irritated at your children's continuous need for your support and feedback? If so, try to identify exactly what it is that bothers you.

2. The next time you feel irritated when your child comes to you with a question or a problem, stop and think about it. Is she really asking something of you that would leave you with less? Or can you open your inner door and let the light shine through you, to your child, enlightening you both?

3. If this is a recurring problem, you can develop an "on the spot" affirmation. You could use the bow and arrow statement, or try to capture in a short sentence your desire to look at demands in a different way. Example:

   This you do not ask of me, but of the Source of Life

   Let me be the window through which the Force may flow

CHILDREN'S QUESTIONS

Children ask a lot of questions. As soon as they learn to say the word "why" they fire that word at their parents with innocent vigor. They ask about the smallest daily occurrence that adults take for granted, as well as about life's inexplicable mysteries.

Although you might feel under siege by your three or six year old, who's "why" sounds like an automatic weapon, this is a very natural phenomenon. So natural, in fact, that you could easily overlook what is in it for parents. When a child asks for instance: "Why do I have germs?" (germs are a very popular subject in our household), there are quite a few options available to you to respond. E.g., I have no idea; That is just the way it is; Let's ask grandma, she is a doctor; They are part of life, just like spiders and flies. And, of course, any reply you make will, again, meet with "Why?" Depending on the time available and the mood you are in at the moment, you will find an answer to brush off the question or to satisfy the child and hopefully yourself, too. There is no need to feel guilty if you do not find the time or energy to fully engage in a conversation at all times. There are times for doing and times for talking and you do not shortcut your children if you postpone your involvement in the matter they bring up. The word "involvement" is actually a key word here, and it points to that which can be of value to parents concerning their children's questions. If you involve yourself with a curious child, you step out of your own limited little circle of assumptions and perspectives and enter the child's world of experience. Immediately it is clear that a brush-off kind of answer is totally insufficient. The child needs a companion on the road to discovery, not a pet answer. Even if you do not know the full answer to all questions, an honest reply is always in order.

In the example of the question about germs, the next question could be: "Why do people get sick from germs?" Again, you could answer in a quick remark aimed at silencing the child, or you could stop and get involved. Why *do* germs make some people sick? Or more general: Why do people get sick at all? And with this question you open the door to new ways of looking at life's situations. You do not have to go out and explore medical data, but rather search for an answer that feels right from within.

When you commit yourself to giving an honest answer, a simple question like the one about germs can be an invitation to look beyond the commonly accepted assumptions and opinions. Even if you are totally confused, as in many instances you surely will be, it seems better to honestly admit that you do not know any more than the child does, than to give an answer you know does not even satisfy yourself.

In this respect it is interesting to consider the oft quoted words by Jesus: "Unless you become as children you will not enter the Kingdom of God." This statement encourages respect for a child's point of view. What a child's point of view has to offer parents is a natural, unspoiled, unprogrammed look at life. Children look at life without preconceptions, prejudices and biased opinions. Entering into their world is rejuvenating. What you can gain from being involved with your children during their quest for the answer to the final "Why?", is a thirst for clarity and an intolerance for ambiguous answers. You can learn from them not to be satisfied with half answers and not to compromise on sincerity.

TV

Newspapers, magazines, radio, TV, video, Internet, interactive multimedia... These sources and others offer instant news and all sorts of information from around the world, continuously. The channels through which you receive it are all right in the center of your home and office. And as soon as you step out of the front door you are confronted with yet another wave of information and impressions: advertisements, announcements, community happenings, meetings, etc. Both, in work and in social life, you are faced with assimilating facts and developments if you want to stay in touch with current events. Clearly it is very easy to get caught up in a never ending quest for the latest, the newest and the hottest. It almost feels that, as long as you are fully informed about the latest development in the areas you are interested in, you are "with-it" and are somehow in charge.

To be focused on external events exclusively, means to lose touch with your inner life. Now you know how you can enhance the development of your inner life, namely by dedication and persistence in finding the truth inside, not outside. This means that you must find room in your mind and time in your day to devote to spiritual life. If you go along with the unending flow of information that encroaches on you from all sides, there will be no time or space left to spend in contemplation. You must set priorities, and choose to deliberately deny the flow of information to engulf you at all times. You need to be fastidious in your choice of information as well as of the time of day and amount of time you allocate to receiving it. Receiving information and interacting with the outside world is not an automation, it is a matter of choice. There is yet another aspect to the information issue, and particularly to television watching, and that is value. As an example, consider the way you select clothing. You wear clothing to protect your body, both from the weather and from unwelcome onlookers, as well as to express your personality. Not just any clothing will do. You do not enter a department-store and grab the first item from the first rack you bump into without regard to size, style, quality and price. When you are a wise buyer you are selective and aware of the value to you personally of the items you buy.

Likewise, you can be selective about the "items" with which you feed your mind. It is easy to just turn the switch and submerge in all kinds of information, from trivial and irrelevant, to biased and harsh. But if you stop and think about it, you realize that what you let enter into your mind will somehow become part of you. If you are not selective about the choice of information you allow to come into your inner room, it will enter unchecked and influence your life in a way you might not want to.

Your mind is the builder of your life. When an intention or an idea is born in the spiritual realm, the mind will act upon it and make the physical manifestation possible. If you crowd your mind with irrelevant and biased information, you do not offer it the best building blocks you are capable of providing. Instead, select the information you feed into your mind on the basis of the value, of the quality it represents to you. The information should not be counteractive to what you hold dearly, as expressed in your framework of ideals, and ideally it should support you and broaden your outlook.

So value, or quality, is a key word, as is quantity. The amount of data that can be assimilated effectively varies from person to person. But at some point you will have to draw a line beyond which harsh and biased information cannot reach you, where you are free of impressions from outside. Not as a place of escape, but as a center, well guarded, to which you turn to connect with your inner being and out of which you come to be in the world.

In addition to the flow of customary information, parents face the need to inform themselves about parenting and child rearing. It is impossible to absorb new information if you have not made room for it. If gaining knowledge in child development is important to you, it means you have to critically look at the amount of time you spend absorbing other information, like the news, documentaries, soaps, commercials, etc. There is a weighing of qualities as well. Information about child rearing in a book by an experienced child psychologist might be of a higher quality to you right now, than some child related article in a women's magazine. What matters is that you make a conscious choice, that you clean up your mental house and do not let unwanted visitors in. That is the way to be "with it", to be in charge.

Parents have an added responsibility. They are the guardians of their children. Particularly during the first seven years of life, children take in information as dry sponges absorb water. They absorb information "as is", they do not yet distinguish between detail and main issue. Their brain cells are still forming and you will want to make sure that this, as well as their overall development, happens in as healthy an environment as possible. Think about their mental house and your role as guardian. Protect them from too much, as well as too harsh impressions and information. The balance that feels right will be different in every household. The point is, that parents become aware of the importance to a growing child to have mental space to come back to again and again, without being over-stimulated by outside impressions.

The medium of which children easily receive an overdose is television. In the western world the amount of time children spend watching television is mind boggling. And boggling the mind is exactly what too much TV watching does to a person, and especially an impressionable child. It can be very convenient to use children's TV programs as baby sitters when you really need to get something done. But the price children pay for a TV overdose is not worth it. TV is a drug. As any drug, it is addictive if exposed to too much and for too long. The symptoms are boredom, lack of curiosity, short attention span, restlessness, and worst of all, the inability to return to the inner being, to experience inner life. Healthy children have no trouble at all to enter into a contemplative state, to reflect on life in their own way. Moreover, they have a very vivid imagination. An overdose of TV kills all that. It blocks the road inward.

Now that you have decided to embark on a spiritual journey yourself and have committed to develop and maintain an active inner life, do not deny your children access to their own inner sanctuary. You, the parent, have the task of measuring the amount and the quality of the information flowing into your living room, to safeguard your children's inner sanctuary, as well as your own.

APPLICATION

TV. Television watching has two aspects. The first aspect is the act of watching. Some psychologists believe that it is better for a child to become bored stiff than to watch TV. When a child is bored it won't be long before she will get fed up with being bored, and will think of something to do. She learns to act upon an uncomfortable feeling. The child is in charge of her decision making. On the other hand, if the TV is switched on right away, the child will never really become acquainted with the feeling of boredom. The child will not learn how to deal with it in a creative way. No creative decision making takes place.

The second aspect of TV watching is the quality of the product. At least some parental guidance in the choice of programs watched by children is called for, to safeguard them from unnecessary harsh influences. Of course, personal preference plays a large role in determining which programs are suitable for children to watch. It is important that parents are aware of the tremendous influence TV programs have on the development of their children. In the area of television watching it is safe to say: Less is more.

It can be hard on a parent to be in the same room with a child who is bored and who begs to watch TV. Keep your educational objectives in mind. Then consult and trust your inner guidance to come up with a solution that will work. See if you can think of a new way to deal with television watching habits. You could watch some programs with your children and talk about them together. Ask them why they like a particular show. Ask them in what way they feel the show connects to their daily life. In the next chapter you will find an example of one way to connect a spiritual ideal with the problem of too much TV watching.

WANTING THE BEST FOR YOUR CHILD

You, like all other parents, wish the best for your children. You select their clothing and toys with dedication, you introduce them to the children of people you like, and you carefully select the person who takes care of them in your absence. And especially in the area of friends, school and teachers, parents usually have a clear vision of the ideal environment for their children.

In your effort to organize and arrange your children's lives you might sometimes forget that they themselves are individuals, as you are. They have their own strengths and abilities, their own ideals and issues to work with. Your children have their own spiritual ideals. Until the time comes when your children will think in terms of ideals and discover their purpose for coming into the world, their guardians have the task to teach by example, and to encourage their children to use their talents and abilities.

In his book about the spiritual laws of life Deepak Chopra explains how he encouraged his children to think in terms of ideals and purpose. His is an uncommon approach, to say the least, and it certainly is thought provoking. He writes:

> *"Again and again, I told them there was a reason why they were here, and they had to find out what that reason was for themselves. From the age of four years, they **heard** this. I also taught them to meditate when they were about the same age, and I told them, "I never, ever want you to worry about making a living. If you're unable to make a living when you grow up, I'll provide for you, so don't worry about that. I don't want you to focus on doing well in*

171

> *school. I don't want you to focus on getting the best grades or going to the best colleges. What I really want you to focus on is asking yourself how you can serve humanity, and asking yourself what your unique talents are. Because you have a unique talent that no one else has, and you have a special way of expressing that talent, and no one else has it." They ended up going to the best schools, getting the best grades, and even in college, they are unique in that they are financially self-sufficient, because they are* **focused on what they are here to give."** *(Author's emphasis)*

"The Seven Spiritual Laws of Success", by Deepak Chopra

It can be hard to give your child room to express who she thinks she is, when that does not rhyme with who you think she is. You feel so much involved and connected with the child and her life, that you have a hard time understanding and accepting that her life unfolds in a way you did not imagine. In this respect it might be good to take a good look at the involvement, to look at the connection parents have with their children. At first, while the child is still in the womb, the connection to the mother is physical and complete. They are one. After birth, the baby depends on physical contact with the parents. Nursing, changing, etc., and of course holding, rocking and cuddling and various other physical expressions of love and care are essential for the baby's growth. By naturally loving your baby, you place yourself under the principle of love. When the child matures the purely physical part of your involvement will diminish and make room for more mental and spiritual involvement. To let the principle of love operate you need to find other expressions of your feeling of love and care, like encouragement, guidance, loyalty, etc. The form of the   loving connection between you and your child will evolve with time; it will change as the child matures.

All parents want to feel connected to their children, and so do all children *if* parents allow them to be partners in their relationship. Imposing your own ideal view of the child's development and   of   the   relationship   will antagonize the child and result in a stagnant and lifeless connection that is doomed.

Whereas one child may clearly indicate the need for parental support   and interest in her life and projects, another child may reject any   parental involvement. Instead, that child might need the parents' encouragement to trust her own judgment to go out into the world and connect with an aspect of Creation that lies outside the family circle. In this case to come under the principle of love means to let go. Letting go is Love in one of its unselfish forms.

10

SPIRITUAL TOOLS FOR ANGER AND DISCIPLINE

Give of your love, give of your patience, give of your long-suffering. For what you <u>give</u>, you possess

Edgar Cayce

ANGER

Being angry at your child

Anger is an emotion parents frequently face. Parents in all kinds of families get angry at their children all the time. Anger in its various expressions can easily become an obstacle in the relationship between you and your child. That is why gaining a broader perspective on anger is so important.

Getting angry with people or situations outside the home is one thing. But to find yourself angered by your

175

very own child, who is so dear to you and is so much a part of you, is an entirely different matter. It can leave you disconcerted and confused. Moreover, the intensity of the anger can be frightening.

In the section on disagreements, you already read about a way to defuse a potential clash of emotions. You learned to mentally step outside the situation for a moment and free yourself from any desired outcome. Then, through centering yourself, you make yourself available to Life, to be directed toward a solution that is best for all involved. You become a channel through which Life can act. This technique can greatly help circumvent all kinds of explosive confrontations. You can teach yourself to be a step ahead, so to speak, in your contact with your children. You can learn to foresee if an exchange is heading in the wrong direction. Instead of being a passive victim of an automatic response, you center yourself so you do not end up in a mine field. Practical and wonderful as this may be, it does not help in instances where you have already become a seething ball of fire. It is not helpful to doubt whether the anger is justified or not. If it is, fine. If it's not, who says so? You are angry anyway. Now that you have become totally furious with your child your focus should be on what you will *do* with all that angry energy. But before looking into that, let's first examine anger more closely.

What exactly is anger?
Anger is strongly felt displeasure that seems to befall us at more or less unpredictable intervals. Moreover, this feeling of strong displeasure demands an immediate expression.

Some people react by shouting out their disapproval. They throw a dish or two, and are over and done with. Entire peoples react in this or similar fashion. On the other hand there are people who do not show their anger and keep a placid facade. This way the effect on the outside world stays minimal. The penned up energy is consumed within. Whole generations of families teach their children to be in control of anger this way. Before long, the children will not be able to recognize and identify their anger anymore. They will become a stranger to part of their being. It may be clear that neither extreme offers the ideal way to soundly express anger. There is no use denying the feeling, to act as if it is not there. Neither is it good to let a sudden rage control your actions only to have to regret it later. Suppressed anger makes you weak, but a temper out of control may be worse.

Anger is an emotion and as such it is one of the fundamental aspects of your being. It cannot be labeled either bad or good. Just as the spices in a dish make it come to life, so do your emotions make you come alive. Too much salt and pepper or too little basil and thyme make for a dish that is out of balance. Salt or pepper in and of themselves are neither good nor bad. The amount in which they are used determines whether the end result is pleasing or unpalatable.

With human emotions it works the same. An overdose of empathy harbors the danger of sentimentality, whereas the right amount allows you to feel compassion. Joy mixed with compassion leads to understanding and peace, while joy without any kind of empathy may lead to hilarity or cynicism. When joy is absent altogether, life is gray and dull. Love, balanced by wisdom and respect, leads to freedom. On the other hand, however, love easily leads to possessiveness if not thus balanced.

When we examine the emotion of anger it becomes clear that an uncontrolled measure of anger will lead to rage and madness. But in the right amount, and in harmony and balance with other ingredients, this spicy herb called anger can perfect an otherwise bland and uninteresting dish. This ingredient does not taste either good or bad. It is just an ingredient, to be used in measure. Anger just is. What matters is what you do with it.

Anger as creative energy

Anger is force. Anger is energy. There is only one source of energy in our universe; there is only one Source from which everything originates. Anger comes from that very same Source. Anger is just an aspect of the full array of emotions through which Creation, through individuals, expresses itself. It is up to each individual to give anger its proper place and expression. You can let it propel you into a rage, or you can measure and control it, and use it as a motivator for creative action. Instead of *reacting in* anger you can learn to *act on* anger in a creative way. Then, instead of experiencing anger as the destructive force everyone is so familiar with, you can experience its creative power. Let's look at an example:

It's Dad's job to give the baby his daily bath. So he takes the plastic tub and places it over the sink of the bathroom counter top to fill it with warm water. Next, he undresses the baby, and, holding the baby in one arm, he reaches for the soap. Enter four year old brother Evan. Evan is curious and wants to see what Dad is up to. So he grabs the rim of the tub to pull himself up on his toes. The tub tips over, spilling the water over Dad and soaking the entire bathroom floor.

A common assumption is that each person reacts to something like this in his or her own way. There is not much you can do about it. It's just the way you are. Well, there *is* something you can do about it, namely decide that you would prefer not to be "on automatic." You *can* choose an alternative, and healthy, way of responding to accidents of this kind. Let's examine possible reactions:

a) Dad swallows his frustration. With a seemingly calm attitude he cleans up the mess, changes, and starts the whole routine over again. But the penned up energy is still there, waiting for the smallest provocation to burst into the open. His wife might call from another room asking if he has seen her keys, and Dad will vent his anger on his wife who is so maddeningly unorganized.

b) Dad swears, throws the baby back in the crib, yells at Evan and anyone who comes close, and emphatically states that bathing babies is women's work and he's not going to do it again.

c) Dad curses, walks over to the crib, tucks in the baby and changes his clothes. He uses the angry energy to clean up the bathroom *fast*. He walks over to the crib and dresses the baby, telling him that today he will have to go without his bath, because Daddy just doesn't feel like trying again. Thinking about the accident, Dad concludes that the counter top in the kitchen is a much more stable surface to hold the bath tub. Evan could not possibly pull it out of balance there. Next time, he decides, he will bathe Junior in the kitchen.

In the first two responses nothing really changes. Dad has only reacted, and the next day, should the tub tip over again, he will respond in similar fashion. In the third response, however, you can see that the anger aroused was used for change. Dad allowed the expression of a certain amount of anger, and then let the anger and the occurrence that aroused it, be an incentive to change this for the better. If anger aroused by such a minor occurrence as water spilled in the bathroom, can be focused in a creative way, imagine what focused anger can accomplish in areas that matter a lot more.

Before you try to determine a new focus for your anger, you will need to know more about what happens now when you are angry. Only when you are fully aware of your current behavior will you be able to change it in a new direction. The "Application" section will help you with this. But before analyzing your own situation, you might like to read the next two sections first.

Anger and your spiritual ideal

Children, by virtue of being children, are vulnerable. Your words and deeds, including your anger, influence them more than you may be aware of. Adults can harness themselves against angry outbursts, but children, by their very nature, are not thus equipped. Angry arrows always hit their heart.

Once you are aware of the destructive potential your uncontrolled angry actions can have on your children you can take up this issue of focusing anger in the right direction. Thus it becomes a matter of personal growth. How do you know the right direction in which to point anger and how do you point it that way? Your spiritual ideal will show you. If anger is a recurring stumbling block in the contact with your children, you could write anger in a section of your ideals target. Relate the ways your children's actions enrage you to your spiritual ideal by formulating mental and physical ideals. Suppose your children's TV-watching habits are a source of irritation and anger. And your spiritual ideal is *To appreciate and bring beauty*. You could connect the two as follows:

spiritual ideal	- *To appreciate and bring beauty*
mental ideals for the parent-child relationship	- *Appreciate child unconditionally*
	- *See the world through child's eyes*
physical ideals, specifically for the recurring problem of defiance of TV watching guidelines	- *Watch TV programs with child and talk about them, to find out what they mean to him*
	- *Discuss guidelines with child and be open to fair arguments*

Your children's priorities sometimes are different from the ones you set for them. Identify with your children and their goals. Try to see objectively where you do not agree. Do not get hung up on your disapproval. Your anger might force their compliance but will most certainly not change their mind. Encouragement and involvement might. Try to understand why the kids acted the way they did. You don't have to sanction it, just see it through their eyes.

Angry parents are role models too

One aspect of anger that you need to consider is that your children will model their behavior after the example you give. If you let your anger take over control and act impulsively, you cannot expect your children to behave differently. On the other hand, your own example of anger consciously focused towards constructive action becomes a powerful model. This, combined with your help in guiding your children to deal with their own anger in a creative way, is a powerful child rearing tool.

But of course you cannot become a perfect example overnight. Even if you are able to focus your anger constructively most of the time, there will be occasions when you blow it. You will miss opportunities to hone your skills and to prove yourself to be a worthy example to your children. At moments like that your children will come to the rescue. Children are very forgiving. They do not like to hold a grudge. Their urge to love you and to be loved by you is too strong. They will gladly wipe your slate clean. Where other people are not likely to give you another chance once you have blown it, your children will.

APPLICATION

1. *Anger.* Think about a time when you felt angry with your child. Think it through in the most objective terms you are capable of. Write down what happened. What triggered the emotion? What did you feel? It may have been powerlessness, frustration, irritation, indignation, etc. Just feel the color and the intensity. Get acquainted with the feeling.

   Analyze the way you responded. Did you try to be tolerant and push aside your feelings, or did you let your rage take over? Was it a reaction or an action?

   It is important to know the answers to these questions. Again, only when you are fully aware of your current behavior will you be able to change it in a new direction. Thinking about these questions will help you in gaining understanding of yourself and of the amount of hot spice you like in the dish called your life.

2. *Anger and your framework of ideals.* For this exercise copy the form on the next page in your notebook, or make a photocopy.

   Think about a recurring situation in your family life that upsets you and makes you angry, each and every time. In a few words write it down in the diagram.

   Look up the personal qualities you wrote down at step 8 of Chapter 2. Write them down in the space provided. Then write down your individual spiritual ideal in the corresponding diagram area.

183

Recurring upsetting
situation:

Personal qualities:

....

....

....

....

....

....

....

....

....

....

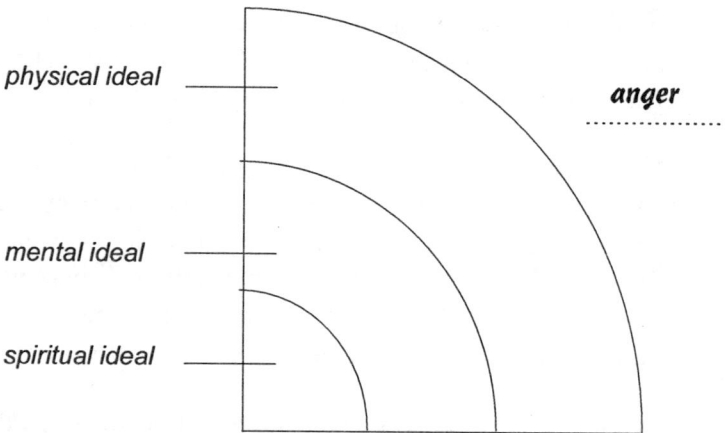

physical ideal

anger

mental ideal

spiritual ideal

Fig. 6

Mental ideals. See if you can come up with an attitude that would express your individual spiritual ideal, possibly combined with a personal quality, that can be of help to you regarding this situation. If no ideas come, imagine what attitude the persons you admire (like the ones mentioned in step 1 of Chapter 2) would have, were they to face this situation. Write down the ideal attitude below. Do not worry if you cannot pinpoint it exactly right now. You might want to use a tentative phrase, and come back to it later to change it.

Physical ideals. Now, think about what you could actually *do*. How can you become actively involved in a creative way? It is very well possible that a physical ideal that expresses focused creative angry energy demands an adjustment of comfortable routines and habits. It calls for vision to enter into a process of trial and error. It takes courage to enact an idea that might be frowned upon by outsiders. Do not worry about that. Think about what matters to you and your family. What counts is to be the door, the channel through which Life's blessings may flow to you and your child, no matter what others may think. So, when you have thought this all through, write down your physical ideal. Remember, it is not set in stone. You can always adjust it later.

DISCIPLINE

The need for discipline

Now that you have looked at the ins and outs of anger and at constructive ways to express it, you can examine another subject that is related to anger, namely behavior control, or discipline. These two are related in the sense that the right amount and quality of behavior control will significantly cut back on instances when anger is aroused.

For instance, when you teach your child to wash his hands before meals, you will not get upset and choke on your chicken when you discover his dirty hands at the dinner table. If your child knows that the deal you have made is one story and one song at bedtime, there will be less temptation for him to fuss. And thus there will be less reason for you to become inpatient and angry. These are just two examples of simple behavior guidelines that have a purely practical ground. Just like traffic lights in the center of town, they help prevent unnecessary collisions. Clearly, for this reason, as well as for personal safety, the need for behavior guidelines cannot be contested. Apart from these, of course, there is the need to teach your child general courtesy and accepted ways of communication. Also, you want to shape your child's behavior on grounds of your personal moral and religious convictions. Moreover, in the case of, for example, television and social life, parents need to shield their children from harmful influences. For various reasons then, clear boundaries for acceptable behavior are necessary.

While the last paragraph discussed the *noun* "discipline," now it is time to look at the *verb* "to discipline." And it is here that styles and opinions vary. Where most parents can agree that some degree of discipline is necessary in daily family life, they differ greatly in the way they believe they should bring that discipline about. It is in the area of disciplining their children that parents run into questions and doubts.

The image that is sometimes used to illustrate the shaping of a child is the image of the pruning of a tree. Dead branches are cut off, as are branches that grow at odd angles, in order for the tree to be healthy, strong and productive. Clear cut and true as this may be for real life trees, for children a different analogy may be more appropriate. Think of a vine that needs a trellis to guide its branches to grow. The trellis offers support and direction for the vine's new growth, so that an abundance of fruit may grow. Eventually, and here the analogy ends, the child will decide for himself where his path will take him and which measures of self control are necessary. But up until that time the parents provide the trellis to guide the child in his growth.

Three levels of understanding

Even though the verb "to guide" sounds more flexible than the verb "to discipline", it does not mean that your child will always agree with it. What do you do when he doesn't? Is there a spiritual way to look at guidance and noncompliance?

As discussed earlier, for the sake of understanding the situation, it helps to distinguish among three levels of reality: the spiritual, mental and physical reality. In the case of guidance and defiance there are three levels of understanding between parents and children, namely a physical, mental and spiritual understanding.

Let's start with the most tangible form, the physical understanding. Your approval of your children's attitudes and actions often finds a reflection in a physical way: a smile on your face, positive comments, tangible rewards, a hug. Material rewards can be very effective in helping kids fulfill various tasks and obligations as well as influencing their attitude. So is your disapproval expressed in physical terms: a frown on your face, negative comments, withholding of privileges, no hug. Withdrawal of objects or treats as a consequence of undesired conduct aids in steering children's behavior in the right direction.

Part of the physical aspect of parental guidance for many is the swat on the buttocks or more severe forms of physical punishment. Although the case of a parent who gives a quick swat on the buttocks reminds me of a lion mother who snaps at her cubs when their play annoys her, it is obvious that other means are available to people to make their point. Some parent educators advise strongly against any kind of physical correction. They believe that even the smallest physically expressed disapproval traumatizes the child. Clearly any form of physical violence is inappropriate, counter productive and totally unacceptable.

The next level is the mental understanding, which is the level of beliefs, attitudes, agreements, rules, routines, etc. It is the level of guidance and encouragement. When your children do not agree with your guidelines, or even rebel, it becomes necessary to analyze the situation and determine:

– if your children can safely divert from your guidelines
– if you can or have to adjust the guidelines to them
– if your children will need to conform to your standards

To illustrate this, consider the following examples:

a) Sandy and Ken have taken their two kids camping. One evening, when they sit down for dinner, their son John announces that he wants to eat his dinner at the fire pit, instead of at the table. Usually, at home, they eat dinner together. Sandy and Ken make an effort to make dinner time a central point in the day. Family members come to dinner from various places and occupations, and afterwards they veer out again. Here at the campground, however, they decide to let John follow his inclination and let him eat his dinner on his own near the fire. In this situation their son's action can safely divert from their guidelines.

b) One of the aspects of camping is shared chores. It is daughter Amy's job to wash the cooking pots and utensils after dinner. Each evening she makes a fuss because she fears she will be too late for a ranger led hike on the park's trails. Sandy likes a job done well and on time, but she recognizes that it would be better to adjust the guidelines. Together they arrive at a different distribution of chores.

c) Since the campground is close to where Ken's uncle lives, the family decides to stop by for a visit. They accept an invitation to stay for dinner. John and Amy ask if they can sit at the fireplace by themselves and have dinner there. Sandy and Ken exchange a glance and decide not to allow that. They feel it would be inappropriate.

Giving an explanation for your guidelines goes a long way in assuring your children's cooperation. Nothing works like a red flag as do seemingly nonsensical rules imposed from above. It is in the case when your children refuse to conform to your fully explained guidelines that you run into problems. How do you make them mind your rules that you have well thought about and that are by no means unreasonable?

It is important to stress again the value of being informed about the issues of child rearing. Knowledge in the area of child development is necessary to be able to estimate how much you can expect of a child at a certain age. Insight into child psychology helps to understand children and the world in which they live. And last but not least, effectively communicating with children is a skill that needs to be learned. Just as driving a car is a skill that requires instruction and practice, so does effectively communicating with children. There are certain "do's and don'ts" of which parents should be aware. It is up to you, the parent, to acquire the necessary insights and skills. For books on these various subjects check the bibliography, the library or a bookstore.

The general thrust of many a book on child rearing is clarity and consistency of guidelines. Guidelines should be unambiguous and apply all the time. They help in making daily life with children run more smoothly, with less irritation on both sides. When guidelines are clear and consistent they are much more effective in achieving their aim: to help children develop in a healthy way to become mature and productive adults. But clear guidelines in and of themselves won't do the trick, either. Your active, positive feedback in the form of praise and appreciation is indispensable for guiding children's behavior.

Let's go back to the third example and see what happens when John and Amy protest and make a fuss when they are told to eat dinner at the table. When you face a potentially embarrassing situation like that you will have to delve deep into your bag of successful strategies, collected from the many sources you have hopefully consulted over the years. Two seemingly opposing perspectives are needed.

First, *acknowledge* their point of view. Remind yourself that you are always on your children's side. It is easy to forget that. You can get caught in the trap of a "perfect parent" raising "perfect children." Then, when reaching for certain educational goals and objectives, you suddenly find that you have become an adversary to your children. Do not forget that you all want the same thing, namely what is best for the children. So, identify with them, empathize with them. See things with their eyes. Meet them where they are. Do not expect them to look over the situation and meet you where you are. In the example of John and Amy this would mean that you tell them that you understand their wish to eat at the fire place because it was so much fun the day before. Clearly *acknowledge* their perspective.

Second, remember that you have the responsibility to provide a trellis to guide your children's development. You will need to *explain* the boundaries of behavior to them in a way they understand.

You are like an intermediary. First you *acknowledge* their wish, and then you *explain* the boundaries of acceptable behavior and ask for their cooperation. Ask for their input on how to bridge the gap between their position and acceptable behavior. In the example this means that you explain to the kids that when you are a visitor in someone else's house, you cannot act as freely as you would in your own. You explain that their uncle likes their company and enjoys having dinner with them. Children are not unreasonable creatures. They have the capacity to empathize with others, once they know others appreciate their point of view, too. When you approach potential confrontations in this two-pronged fashion (acknowledge and explain) you will see that laying down rules and forcefully implementing them is necessary far less frequently, if at all.

Finally, to get back to the three levels of understanding between parents and children, there is the deepest level of understanding, the spiritual understanding. In my own life, once in a while there are moments when I feel such a deep understanding and connection with my child, that we seem to move together in perfect synergy, like two dolphins in the sea. Both of us sense the mood and anticipate each other's movements. Neither discipline nor parental guidance belong in this world. When moving in synergy like that, there is no need for one to direct or guide the other. Those moments don't last long and they cannot be brought about by force. They can, however, be sought after, and worked for, and when they happen, they offer the ultimate in happiness and peace.

Maybe, when each of us individually and humankind as a whole have grown in spirit, people are able to stay on the plane of spiritual understanding for longer periods of time. Then, even the smallest physical correction, like pulling a child away from the stove, will not be necessary because of improved communications. Insults and other kinds of mental abuse will not have to occur either.

Most of the time shaping and steering your children's development take place on the mental level, namely teaching of good habits, encouraging positive attitudes and actions, etc. However, shaping and steering are not the only ways to guide your children. It is important to remember that your personal attitude towards life and your personal conduct influence your children in a measure that cannot be overestimated. When your child is faced with a parental guideline that you violate yourself, he hears "yes" and "no" at the same time. The child is left without a clear idea what he is supposed to do. More often than not, he will do what he feels and sees, rather than what he hears. He will model his behavior after yours. When you practice what you preach, there will be far less need for preaching. So again, like in the case of expressing anger, your own example will do most of the work.

APPLICATION

1. *Discipline.* What is your position on the discipline/parental guidance issue? Have you informed yourself about it? Do you follow your intuition? Do you basically repeat what your parents taught you? Is child guidance an issue you like to think about at all?

2. Think of an area in the contact with your child where you face the recurring problem of protest, whining or disobedience. Depending on you child's age, it can range from touching the plants, and crossing the street, to doing chores around the house and homework. Describe your issue. Think about your priorities in this matter. Think about what really counts. Then determine whether:
   - your child can safely divert from your guidelines
   - you really have to adjust to him
   - your child will have to comply with your standard

In the case of touching the plants, there might be one plant he can safely explore. Then, as soon as you see him heading for the plants, you direct him to that particular plant. Adjusting to him would be to either take all plants out of his reach, or to stay with him while he explores. When there are no two ways about it, and he simply cannot touch the plants, period (when visiting for instance), you sympathize with him, acknowledging his need to feel the leaves. Then you explain in understandable language why this is not possible right here and now. See if he is interested in an alternative, like colored paper or cloth. But be firm about the boundaries of acceptable behavior.

3. If you are certain that your child needs to conform with your guidelines, you try to gain as full an understanding of the situation as possible. What is the physical reality? For example:

plants	: he rips the leaves
street	: he wanders on the busy street
chores/	: he does not do it
homework	

Since a solution needs to be found on the mental level, the level of child guidance, information from the spiritual level can be of help. The spiritual realities of these examples are:

plants	: he needs to connect with an aspect of Creation
street	: he needs to get to know the world and explore freely
chores/ homework	: right to self-determination. He needs to decide for himself which activities are worthy of his attention and effort

4. Can you determine what the spiritual reality of your issue is?

5. On the mental level, the level where guiding children finds expression, acknowledgment and explanation are the key words. Write down the words you will use to let your child know that you *acknowledge* his perspective, that you understand him, that you are on his side. Do not forget to meet him at the place he is now.

6. Write down the words you will use to *explain* to your child why you cannot grant his wish. Call upon his ability to empathize with other people (e.g. Grandma spends a lot of time caring for her flowers), to recognize potential danger (a car could run you over), or work towards long term objectives (education) and fairness (shared chores). Ask for his cooperation and input in finding a solution.

   Present possible alternative ways to let him express his spiritual need. Alternatives for the above examples:

plants	: let him tear paper; give him pile of rags
street	: hold his hand; let him roam in the park
chores	: give him choice; let him decide when
home-work	: within boundaries let him decide when and where, always being supportive and encouraging

EPILOGUE

You have come to the end of this book. A book that encourages you to look upon parenting as an opportunity for personal spiritual growth. You have read many examples that show how spirituality can be applied in daily life situations with kids. These examples demonstrate the positive impact applied spirituality will have on both your children and yourself.

You have learned how to use various spiritual tools. The setting of ideals and the resulting framework of ideals is an important instrument that works like a compass. It allows you to set a course and it provides you with clear feedback on your progress.

You have seen how various tools help you to embark on a journey into the spiritual world. An active inner life is essential to be able to brave the storms that parenthood has in store for you. The tool called prayer is the first tool needed on the road to inner life. Like a brush it clears out your inner chamber and makes room for the Creative Forces. Meditation forms the key that opens the door to admit the Creative Forces. To help you locate both the door and the key in hectic or upsetting times, you make use of affirmations. They serve as little hand drawn maps that point you in the right direction. They are little "instructions for use," to help you remember who you are and what you are about. Next, inner guidance is the two-way lens that first beams in on helpful information within, and then projects that information as a ray of light onto the matter at hand.

In addition to that you have three other devices at your disposal, namely three new perspectives that work like frames. The first frame reminds you to look for the message in each experience. The second one helps you analyze the issue to see if a stumbling block can be made into a stepping stone. Finally, the third frame reminds you that right and wrong choices do not exist. What does exist is the right spirit in which to make a choice. These three "frames of mind" allow you to look at circumstances in a new way and distinguish the spiritual reality beyond the visible appearance.

Every day, parents face issues like the ones discussed in this book and more. What should you do when you and your spouse continually disagree on parental decisions? What about in-laws that interfere with the rearing of your children in a way you do not approve of? How can you best deal with a family situation where one child needs more time and attention than the others because of a special problem? What about the issues of divorce and integration of step family members?

First, whatever the issue you face, get informed about it. Know where you stand. Check the library and the bookstore for helpful information. Take a class in child development or parental guidance at the local community college. Join or start a support group if the issue is of great concern to you. It is invaluable to get feedback and fresh perspectives from other people in similar situations. Look for ways to encourage and receive encouragement from others. There is nothing like a pat on the back or a heartfelt hug from someone who knows exactly how you feel because he or she has been there.

Second, try to look at the issue from a spiritual perspective. See if you can devote a section of your target of ideals to the matter at hand. Can you determine a new attitude toward it that flows naturally from your individual spiritual ideal? Armed now with sure knowledge about your own individual truth you will no longer feel at a loss in the face of trial and tribulation. At your quiet time, and at any time you feel you need it, turn within. Release your anxiety through prayer, wait for the Creative Forces to flow through you, and consult your inner guidance. As long as you keep the lifeline to your center vibrant and strong there is no reason to feel hesitant, disheartened or intimidated. Think about the message the experience holds for you. Analyze the problem and search for a way to turn it into an asset. And finally remember that what matters is the right spirit behind your attitudes and actions.

Of course, problems will not vanish overnight as if by magic. But your perspective and attitude have changed. Now the troubles you face will no longer be debilitating or make you feel inadequate. The instruments and devices of your spiritual toolbox will enable you to find the inner path to right action. While you will look for information and support from outside, you know that the solution that is right for you will have to come from inside. Within is found the fount of life.

Living with children can be a joyful, enriching experience when you are consciously connected on three levels: physically, by living together and sharing activities; mentally, through encouragement, guidance and planning; and spiritually, by loving your children and sharing with them your life's deepest truth, your spiritual ideal.

APPENDIX

Setting of Ideals Worksheet

Date:
Core group of personal qualities (from step 8, Chapter 2):

....

....

....

....

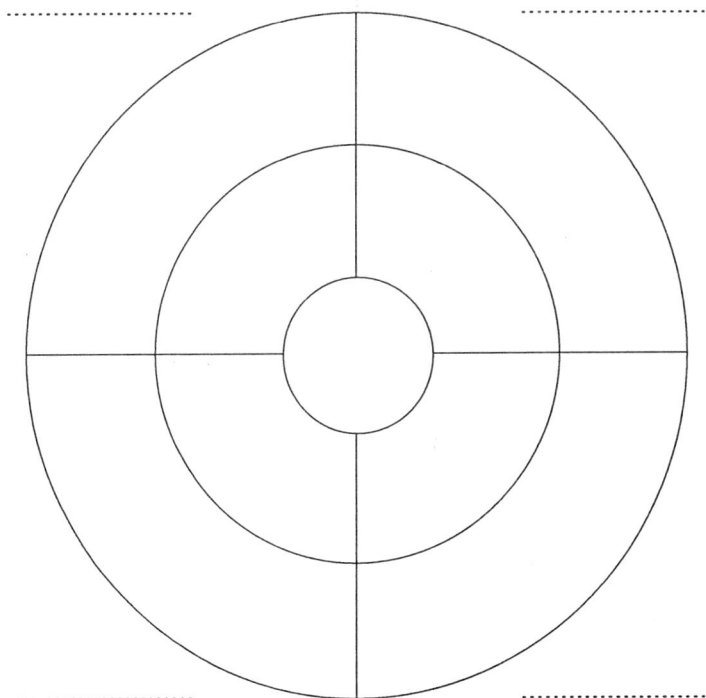

BIBLIOGRAPHY
suggestions for further reading

SPIRITUAL LIFE

THE BIBLE - Any translation

BHAGAVAD GITA - Any translation

A SEARCH FOR GOD, BOOK I AND II, A.R.E. Press, 1992
Guide to spiritual growth, consisting of two times twelve lessons for individual or group use. Based on Edgar Cayce's work

CONSCIOUS UNION WITH GOD, by Joel Goldsmith, First Carol Publishing Group, 1990
Guide to spiritual life and spiritual healing, written in a personable tone

THE INFINITE WAY, by Joel Goldsmith,   Willing Publ. Co., 1976
Guide on the spiritual path. Other titles by Goldsmith also highly recommended

THE PROPHET, by Kahlil Gibran, Random House, 1995
Poems that reveal the truth in life

OCEAN OF WISDOM, by the 14th Dalai Lama of Tibet, Harper & Row, 1989
Nobel Prize acceptance speech, interviews and quotes

A COURSE IN MIRACLES
Foundation for Inner Peace, 1975
Guide to inner peace with year long daily lessons

SPIRITUAL PRINCIPLES

YOUR LIFE. WHY IT IS THE WAY IT IS AND WHAT YOU CAN DO ABOUT IT, by Bruce McArthur, A.R.E. Press, 1993
Clear exposition of spiritual principles and the way they work. Highly recommended

THE EDGAR CAYCE HANDBOOK FOR CREATING YOUR FUTURE, by Mark A. Thurston and Ch. Fazel, A.R.E. Press, 1992
Explanation of spiritual principles as put forward in the work by American psychic Edgar Cayce

THE SEVEN SPIRITUAL LAWS OF SUCCESS: A PRACTICAL GUIDE TO THE FULFILLMENT OF YOUR DREAMS, by Deepak Chopra, Amber-Allen Publishing, 1994
Introduces seven basic laws of life. Based on his earlier book "Creating Affluence"

MEDITATION AND PRAYER

THE ART OF MEDITATION, by Joel S. Goldsmith, Harper & Row, 1956
Insights into meditation

PRACTICING THE PRESENCE, by Joel S. Goldsmith, Harper & Row, 1958
On spiritual development

MEDITATION AND THE MIND OF MAN, by Herbert B. Puryear and Mark A. Thurston, A.R.E. Press, 1987
Meditation and psychology

CREATIVE MEDITATION, by Rich. Peterson, A.R.E. Press, 1990
Step by step explanation of how to meditate, receive inner guidance and set ideals

MEDITATION, GATEWAY TO LIGHT, by Elsie Sechrist, A.R.E. Press, 1987
Guide to meditation. Includes a section on the spiritual centers of the body

HEALING, AURA ,CHAKRAS

HANDS OF LIGHT. A GUIDE TO HEALING THROUGH THE HUMAN ENERGY FIELD, by Barbara Ann Brennan, Bantam Books, 1988
Extensive explanation of the human aura, the role of the chakras and healing

AURAS, by Edgar Cayce, A.R.E. Press, 1987
Color by color explanation

HEALING THROUGH MEDITATION AND PRAYER, by Meredith Ann Puryear, A.R.E. Press, 1978
Guide to prayer and meditation, and to healing through prayer

PARENT GUIDANCE, CHILD DEVELOPMENT AND CHILD REARING

LOVING YOUR CHILD IS NOT ENOUGH. POSITIVE DISCIPLINE THAT WORKS, by Nancy Samalin, Viking Penguin, 1987
Practical guide to child guidance, offering new ways to communicate effectively with children. Highly recommended

P.E.T., PARENT EFFECTIVENESS TRAINING, by Thomas Gordon, Peter Wyden, 1970
Practical guide to change the way we communicate with children. Other titles by Gordon also recommended

THE ABSORBENT MIND, by Maria Montessori, Delta, 1967
In-depth look at how the mind of a child functions, written by a groundbreaking doctor and educator. All of Montessori's books are highly recommended

THE HURRIED CHILD. GROWING UP TOO FAST TOO SOON, by David Elkind, Addison-Wesley Publishing Co., 1981
Explains the detrimental effects of not allowing children to develop at their own natural pace

LIBERATED PARENTS - LIBERATED CHILDREN, by Adele Faber and Elaine Mazlish, Grosset & Dunlap, 1974
Suggestions and specific techniques for communicating with children, written by two mothers

HOW TO TALK SO KIDS WILL LISTEN AND LISTEN SO KIDS WILL TALK, by Adele Faber and Elaine Mazlish, Rawson-Wade, 1980
Suggestions and specific techniques for communicating with children, written by two mothers

HOW CHILDREN FAIL, by John C. Holt, Pitman, 1964
A critique on our society's customary way of communicating with children by an advocate of home schooling

FOR YOUR OWN GOOD: HIDDEN CRUELTY IN CHILDREARING AND THE ROOTS OF VIOLENCE, by Alice Miller, Farrar, Straus & Giroux, 1983
In this book, as in her other titles, Miller explains how children are traumatized by "poisonous pedagogy," where harsh parental discipline is passed on from generation to generation

BETWEEN GENERATIONS, by Ellen Galinsky, Times Books, 1981
How parents change and grow through the demands of the developing child

206

BIG SPIRITS, LITTLE BODIES. PARENTING YOUR WAY TO WHOLENESS, by Linda Crispell Aronson, A.R.E. Press, 1995
Shows how daily life with children spurs you on to personal spiritual growth

EDGAR CAYCE'S READINGS ON HOME AND MARRIAGE: THERE WILL YOUR HEART BE ALSO, by William and Gladys McGary, Bantam Books, 1987
A blending of personal experience and concepts from Edgar Cayce's work, with chapters on many aspects of family life, written by two physicians

DREAMS

DREAMS AND SPIRITUAL GROWTH: A CHRISTIAN APPROACH TO DREAMWORK, by Louis M. Savary, Patricia H. Berne and Strephon Kaplan Williams, Paulist Press, 1984
Includes 37 dreamwork techniques

GETTING HELP FROM YOUR DREAMS, by Henry Reed, InnerVision Publishing, 1985
Dream guide by an Edgar Cayce specialist

DREAMS: TONIGHT'S ANSWERS FOR TOMORROW'S QUESTIONS, by Mark A. Thurston, Harper & Row, 1988
Dream guide by an Edgar Cayce specialist

GENERAL

THERE IS A RIVER: THE STORY OF EDGAR CAYCE, by Thomas Sugrue, A.R.E. Press, 1990
Biography of Edgar Cayce. Includes a chapter on the philosophy underlying Cayce's work

THE EDGAR CAYCE PRIMER. DISCOVERING THE PATH TO SELF-TRANSFORMATION, by Herbert B. Puryear, Bantam Books, 1982
In-depth view of the psychology and philosophy of Edgar Cayce. Great introduction to those new to Edgar Cayce

THE ROAD LESS TRAVELED. A NEW PSYCHOLOGY OF LOVE, TRADITIONAL VALUES AND SPIRITUAL GROWTH, by M. Scott Peck, Simon & Schuster, 1978
An in-depth study in clear language of the role of love and grace in healing within the psychotherapist-patient relationship. Many insightful references to the parent-child relationship. Highly recommended

HOMESICK FOR HEAVEN, by Walter Starcke, Guadelupe Press, 1988
A spiritual autobiography in which Starcke relates his personal transformation

A BROADER VISION. PERSPECTIVES ON THE BUDDHA AND THE CHRIST, by Richard H. Drummond, A.R.E. Press, 1995
Study of common themes in philosophy, ministry and life of the Buddha and the Christ by a Christian theologian and student of Buddhism

MISTER GOD, THIS IS ANNA, by Fynn, Ballantine Books, 1974
Moving account of the life of Anna, an extraordinary child who had a direct line to God. Written by her close friend Fynn

THE CELESTINE PROPHECY, by James Redfield, Warner Books, 1993
A novel. A captivating account of a man's journey to discover universal principles

RELATED WEB SITES

http://www.are-cayce.com
Site of the A.R.E. (Association for Research and Enlightenment). The A.R.E. preserves and studies the more than 14.000 readings given by Edgar Cayce, America's best documented psychic. The readings respond to questions about physical ailments, mental concerns and spirituality

http://www.worldprayer.org/index.html
An outreach of "The Best Is Yet to Be!" television ministry. Site for various prayers as well as prayer requests

http:/www.sequel.net/peace/welcome.htm
Site of "Peace Ideas", a publication that seeks to help individuals to become active participants in the realization of lasting peace. It contains suggestions condensed from the writings of authors from all over the world

http://newciv.org/worldtrans/spirevol.html
Site of "Spiritual Evolution", information and tools for times of accelerating consciousness

http://nen.sedona.net/nhne/index.html
Site of "NewHeavenNewEarth", contact point for people seeking a new way of life on our planet, with many links to other sites

http://www.gaiamind.org
Site of "The Gaiamind Project", dedicated to the idea that humanity is the Earth becoming aware of itself. With links to other spiritual and new-age web sites

http://www.spiritlink.com

Site for exploring inner space with many links to spiritual and new-age web sites

http://www.positiveparenting.com

Site of "Positive Parenting", with helpful articles on child rearing and many links to related sites

http.//family.starwave.com

Site of "Family Planet", a resource for parents with articles on child guidance, related news and events calendar. Well-known experts answer your questions on-line

http://www.users.dircom.co.uk

Site of "Exploring Parenthood", the leading organization in Britain dedicated to parents

http://uc2.unicall.be/ascad

Site of "Pacific Spirit", dedicated to practical spirituality in daily life with children. With parent guidance and on-line advice from writer and counselor Johanna van Zwet

GLOSSARY

To define physical places and objects is a manageable task. Describing ideas related to the mind (e.g., attitudes, beliefs, drives) becomes a little harder. Different people may have different conceptions of one and the same notion. But still, some kind of consensus can be reached. It is not surprising that in the case of phrasing spiritual notions we tread slippery ice. The spiritual world after all is a world beyond words. Nevertheless, some degree of clarity is necessary. The following list is not a dictionary in the usual sense. It applies to this book at this point in time.

Affirmation   A declaration of truth, a statement that captures the essence of a thought that quickens the mind and soul

Creative Forces Name for the unnamable source of all

Framework of ideals

Design that connects spiritual, mental and physical ideals. The framework of ideals forms a tool to express inner intent in the physical world. The idea of setting ideals spiritually, mentally and physically is found in Edgar Cayce's work. *Also called*: Set of ideals, Target of ideals

Ideal   An honorable or worthy principle. In this book the word is used in connection with the framework of ideals

Mental ideal   Ideal that flows from and expresses the chosen individual spiritual ideal, and relates to the world of thoughts, attitudes, plans, beliefs, etc. Part of the framework of ideals

Physical ideal   Ideal that flows from and expresses both the chosen individual spiritual ideal and mental ideals, and relates to the world of matter and action. Part of the framework of ideals

Setting of ideals spiritually, mentally and physically

Process of defining individual spiritual, mental and physical ideals

Spiritual Ideal   A thought that represents the highest understanding of truth and purpose. Part of the framework of ideals

Universal ideal   The one spiritual ideal humans share with the entire Creation, namely to be one with Spirit (God, the Creative Forces)

Working level spiritual ideal

Individually chosen spiritual ideal as opposed to the one universal spiritual

INDEX

Author's Note

I would love to hear from you. Send me your comments, reactions and suggestions. Let me know which ideas were helpful to you, and what difficulties you may have encountered. You can reach me at the address below. Thank you.

Johanna van Zwet

c/o Ascad Communications
15732 Los Gatos Blvd., #306
Los Gatos, CA 95030

e-mail: ascad@unicall.be

website: http://uc2.unicall.be/ascad

Order Form

Fax/voice mail orders: Call (408) 490-2794. Have your card ready.

E-mail orders: ascad@unicall.be

Postal orders: Ascad Communications,
                        15732 Los Gatos Blvd., #306,
                        Los Gatos, California 95030, USA

Please send the following books:
I understand that within 14 days I may return any books for a full refund -
for any reason, no questions asked.

[   ] copies of <My Kids Grow and So Do I> by Johanna van Zwet,
for $US 16.95 plus $US 4.55 S/H per copy.

(Canadian orders: $CDN 24.95 plus $CDN 5.95 S/H per copy)

Sales tax:
Please add 8.25% for books shipped to California addresses.

Shipping:
Shipping charges are Book Rate. Surface shipping may take three to four
weeks. For Air Mail please add $US 3.10 (*$CDN 4.50*) per book.

Payment:

☐ Check (make check payable to Ascad Communications)

☐ Credit Card: ☐ VISA   ☐ MasterCard
     Credit Card Number: _____
     Cardholder's Full Name: _____
     Expiration Date: _____/____

Call and order now!